A PICTURESQUE TALE OF PROGRESS

By Olive Beaupré Miller

Assisted by Harry Neal Baum

BEGINNINGS

PART II

THE BOOK HOUSE FOR CHILDREN

CHICAGO

PRINTED IN U.S.A.

CONTENTS

LIST OF MAPS

THE PICTURE ON THE COVER *is from the magnificent palace of the warlike Assyrian king, Ashur-nazir-apal II. In the last days of his reign, Assyria was at peace, and Assyrian artists for the first time recorded the doings of history.*

This picture shows a tribute of monkeys. Two short and stocky captives of the great king are clad in heavily fringed, Assyrian dress with shoes upturned in true Hittite fashion. The hands of the first tribute bearer are raised in supplication to the king. He is dressed in a long fringed robe and a conical headdress of winding folds.

On the shoulder of the second tribute bearer, a monkey is crouched, with his slender arm over the rope, and his tiny hand clutching the fillet which binds his master's hair. Another monkey is led by a rope, but he rises on his hind legs and looks regretfully backward. Monkey nature was never more faithfully portrayed.

I

Babylonia, the Land of Two Rivers

The City-Kingdoms of Sumer

(FROM ABOUT 5000 B.C. to 2772 B.C.)

In 3500 B.C. when history was dawning by the Nile, there was in far away Asia, all unknown to Egypt, another intelligent nation working out the great problems of culture and civilization. Already their King and Queen were holding magnificent court, sitting in splendid robes, wearing rare golden crowns and surrounded by beautiful things, while musicians entertained them by playing on golden lyres. This country was the land called Sumer lying far to the north and to the east of the Nile Valley beyond the Red Sea and Arabia. Men for centuries thought that civilization began in Egypt but today no one can be certain; for in the

To the left an alabaster statuette of a Sumerian woman of 3300 B.C., wearing a sheepskin dress. Found at Ur by C. Leonard Woolley. Next, the Lord of Fertility and the Mother Goddess with her little son. The fact that these are divine beings is indicated by the enlargement of their eyes in striking distinction from the human types shown in the other heads. Certain classes of Sumerian men wore long hair and a beard, other classes including priests shaved face and head. Found at Tel Asmar by the Oriental Institute, University of Chicago.

The royal family at a feast, the men with clean-shaven faces and round bald heads. They wear the scalloped Sumerian skirt with naked upper bodies. Note the musical instrument at the upper right corner, and the procession of servants with cattle, goats, sheep, fish and bundles of food for the feast. (A companion to the panel on page 13.)

earliest days when Egyptians were discovering writing and gaining skill in the arts, these people in the land of Sumer were learning to do the same things in a totally different way but with no less skill and success.

In the valley between two great rivers, the Ti'gris and the Eu-phra'tes, where As-syr'i-a and Bab'y-lo'ni-a were later to rise to power, there stretched a low-lying plain over which the rivers on their way to the Persian Gulf left rich deposits of mud just as the Nile did in Egypt. For a hundred and sixty-five miles above the Persian Gulf, the long narrow Plain of Shinar lay between these two rivers, rich and green and level, with nothing to relieve its endless flat monotony save a grove of palm trees here and there silhouetted against the sky.

Now Egypt had always been shut off from neighboring tribes by the Cataracts and the desert—her people were left much alone to live in comparative peace; but in the Land of Two Rivers, there dwelt an endless confusion of tribes, mountain people and desert people, constantly striving together to gain the farm-lands and the pastures. The earliest settlers in the valley were mountain-folk, called the Su-me'-

rians, who had swarmed down out of their heights to live on the fertile plain. Thus their land was first called Su′mer.

In the growing cities of Sumer rows of flat-roofed houses, made of sun-baked clay brick with walls more than ten feet high, rose along narrow lanes. Threading their way through the canyons formed by these glistening walls as they angled a way up the street, men with close-shaven heads, round and bald as a baby's, went about the business of life dressed in oddly flounced and scalloped little skirts. Some led cattle to market, others carried great bundles fastened on their backs and steadied by straps round their foreheads. Here a soldier passed in his trim felt military cape and his close-fitting copper helmet, there walked a woman dressed in sheep's fleece with a turban around her head, and thundering along up the street on solid wooden discs of wheels, came a clumsy wooden chariot drawn by four donkeys abreast.

People in the land of Sumer had long ago learned to weave cloth and in their busy market places, one could find beauti-

A Su-me′rian King at war, 3500 B.C. In the top row he marches before his chariot while naked prisoners are driven before him that he may decide their fate. In the middle row light-armed skirmishers engage the foe and behind come a phalanx of heavy-armed troops with copper helmets, short stabbing spears and heavy cloaks of felt.
In the bottom row, four-wheeled chariots, each drawn by four asses and containing a driver and a warrior, advance over fallen foes. The wheels are an interesting feature, for Sumerians first invented the wheel to take the place of sledges. A remarkably beautiful inlay of shell, lapis lazuli, and pink limestone found at Ur by C. Leonard Woolley.

ful objects finely wrought of gold, all kinds of inlay work,
and skilful carvings on stone. Not a well-to-do man in
Sumer but owned, for the stamping of letters or business and
legal documents, his small cylindrical seal, delicately cut in
stone with tall slim graceful figures in most artistic lines.
To such a degree of culture the Sumerians had arrived, while
the nearest neighbors around them could scarcely mould a
mud doll. Moreover they had developed their civilization
alone, knowing nothing in those days of Egypt, though
they were learning to write at just about the same time as
the people in the valley of the Nile. Writing began in Sumer
just as it did in Egypt with making pictures of objects; but
the bald-headed scribes of Sumer writing business documents or keeping the temple records, instead of drawing on
paper or carving their pictures on stone, pressed the wedge-
shaped end of a reed down into tablets of clay which they
afterwards baked in the fire till they became hard like pottery. Therefore these writing-pictures were made up of
wedge-shaped lines like this one meaning star ✳ and such
wedge-shaped inscriptions are called cuneiform writing.

Shinar, the original Sumer; Babylon; As'shur, and the growth of the Assyrian Empire. See p. 19; V. I, 182, 187.

To the left Queen Shub-ad's splendid golden headdress (3000 B.C.), discovered in her grave at Ur by Mr. C. Leonard Woolley, Director of the Joint Expedition of the British Museum and University of Pennsylvania. The head and wig were modelled by Mrs. Woolley over the cast of a skull of the period. Next, a bull's head in gold with hair and beard of lapis lazuli, the beard being the sign of a god.
To the right a wig of gold, the wavy lines engraved with faultless regularity. The holes around the rim are for fixing the wadded lining. The wig is shown on a head because it was meant to be worn either as a helmet or a ceremonial headdress. (All articles on this page were found by Mr. Woolley at Ur.) For Ur see pages 88–89.

Commerce and trade in Sumer, with all the bustle of life, centered about the temples, those great tall zig'gu-rats or towers of receding square piles which rose in imposing dignity like to some holy mountain in the center of a sacred enclosure. Before the Sumerian tribes had come down into the plain, their gods had dwelt on the loftiest summits in their highlands and when they settled in the valleys, the worshipers feared these gods would grieve in such flat lowlands with homesick longing for the hills. And so they built for them great towering artificial mountains of stone; these pyramids of their temples, where in shrines at the top, their gods might still live on high.

The chief priest was really the king; he collected taxes, built canals, decided cases of justice, and even engaged in trade, and gradually these priest-kings came to live in very great splendor as

Exquisite golden dagger of Ur. Made of solid gold with blue lapis handle. The sheath is covered with an intricate filigree of marvelous workmanship. (See page 87.)

their cities grew in wealth. Powerful lines of city Kings ruled at Kish and Ur, at Lar'sa and at Nip-pur. And when these great Kings died they were buried in sumptuous style, not only with all their belongings and the glory of headdress or crown, but with a mighty slaughter of men and women of the court and of oxen to draw their chariots in the world to which they were going.

When the great Queen Shub-ad died, she took with her to her tomb her chariot and team of asses, three royal grooms to drive her, six bearers of golden lances and arrows, women singers and harp players with beautiful golden harps, her gaming board to amuse her, her wardrobe, her jewels and ornaments, her gold and silver vessels and utensils of copper and stone. And a powerful King of the time, still more magnificent in his mighty demand for companions and a proper royal retinue to escort him to the underworld had sacrificed in his tomb nine ladies of the court, fifty male attendants and six of his finest oxen to draw his two wooden chariots. All drawn up in place at the time of the great King's burial, they were killed in perfect order and found five thousand years later in the very place where each fell.

Splendid was the civilization that grew up here in Sumer, in spite of the barbarism displayed in the burial of its princes. Sumer could equal Egypt in what through persistent thinking, love of beauty and skill it had gained in knowledge from the chaos of knowing nothing.

Milking customs of ancient Sumer. To the left men pour the milk into jars, strain it, and work it into butter or cheese. At the right a calf is tied to its mother by a rope. A temple frieze from Tel-el-Obeid (4300 B.C.).

Sargon I, the Ruler of Sumer and Akkad
(2772 B.C. TO 2717 B.C.)

Always the green fertility of the Valley of the Two Rivers tempted wild tribes from the desert and the barren mountain-sides to seize the food supply. Raid after raid occurred, and at length black-bearded herdsmen, roving tribes of Sem'ites from the rocky Arabian desert, settled to the north of Sumer and called their country Ak'kad.

For years the Semites were wanderers and built themselves no cities but lived in tents as their fathers had, roaming hither and yon wherever they could find pasture.

In their wanderings, now and then, they came to the southern cities, those wonderful cities of Sumer. Beholding the riches of Ur, of Larsa, and of Nippur, the herdsmen longed to possess them.

Then Sar'gon, the Semite, the humble son of a low-born mother, made himself King of Akkad and the first great Sem-it'ic chief.

Sargon taught his soldiers to fight with bows and arrows, instead of crouching back of shields and using only spears as was the Sumerian custom. Setting forth with his army, he fell on the men of Sumer, who fought in remarkable order, the warriors close together with overlapping shields.

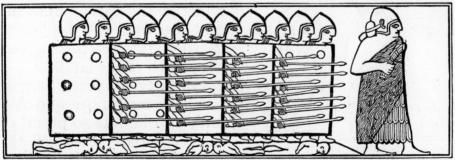

A Sumerian City-King, leading a phalanx of his troops who advance in remarkable order behind square overlapping shields. The Sumerians were the first people in the world to go into battle in order. Such discipline was unknown in Egypt at this time. The art of war began in Sumer. (Found at Lagash, now in the Louvre, Paris.)

The wandering Semitic tribes had no organized troops and no discipline. They fought hit or miss as they chose in sharp contrast to the orderly Sumerians. The Semites were bearded and had bushy hair in contrast to the clean-shaven Sumerians. This distinction lasted for many years after the Semites conquered the Sumerians. See pages 87-88. (A Semitic stone carving.)

Arrows flew further than spears; so in spite of the well-ordered charges made by the warriors of Sumer, Sargon defeated the King of Ur and conquered all the land.

East across the Tigris to the mountain land of Elam with its narrow, treacherous passes, he sent his victorious soldiers and west up the Euphrates to the shores of the Mediterranean; and so at last he ruled all the vast Land of Two Rivers, all the cities of Sumer, and all the tribes of herdsmen who pastured their sheep in Akkad.

The half-wild Semites wandered no more, but settled down and built cities; they turned to the Sumerians to learn how to read and write, how to farm and carry on business, and how to arrange their armies in orderly formation.

Men of the Semite tribes married Sumerian women. On the streets of Sumer and Akkad were seen both the dark-bearded Semites in their flowing woolen robes and the beardless, bald-headed Sumerians, clad only in ruffled skirts. Gradually Semitic replaced the early Sumerian and became the language heard everywhere throughout the length of the land.

A Sumerian man with shaven head, monstrous beaked nose and flounced skirts (a stone carving) and the finely carved figure of a woman, probably Semitic, her hair in a twisted loop, her garment a long, fringed shawl. (A seal.)

For fifty-six years Sargon I ruled over Sumer and Akkad, and he was so proud of his deeds that he caused the tale of his life to be written on tablets of clay. A part

Sargon's Semitic mother entrusts her son to the river, a scene resembling the tale of the babe Moses. The background is typical of the fertile Plain of Shinar. Round basket-boats of rushes are still used on the Euphrates.

of this tale resembles the Bible story of Moses, the babe.

"Sargon, the powerful king, King of Akkad, am I;
My mother was of low degree, my father I did not know.
The brother of my father dwelt in the mountain;
My city was As-u-pi-ra'ni, on the banks of the river Euphrates;
My humble mother conceived me; in secret she brought me forth.
She placed me in a boat, a basket-boat of rushes; with pitch she closed my door.
She gave me to the river, which did not rise above me;
The river bore me along; it carried me to Akki, Akki, the irrigator.
Akki, the irrigator, reared me as his own son.
Akki, the irrigator, appointed me his gardener.
While I was his gardener, Ishtar, (mother goddess) looked on me with love,
In four years I ruled the kingdom."

For some two hundred years, the descendants of Sargon I ruled in Sumer and Akkad. Sargon's son, Naram-Sin, a man of wisdom and strength, built temples, roads, and canals, and brought the cities still closer together under one central rule.

But it came to pass in time that the city of Ur rebelled, threw off the yoke of the Semites, and once again created

Stele of Naram-Sin, son of Sargon (2800 B. C.). The king has pursued the enemy into a mountain stronghold in Elam. In military dress, carrying his bow and arrows, he ascends a mountain, followed by soldiers with standards and spears. His enemies, killed in masses slide down the wooded mountain slope. One just before him, begs for mercy while the king lowers his weapon to show that he grants the conquered their lives. In the sky are two stars of Ishtar, the protectress of Akkad and the goddess of war. The earliest great Semitic work of art, done with realism and skill and the first attempt to show landscape, mountains and trees.

a great Sumerian empire under the rule of her kings. Henceforth for five hundred years, there were priest-kings in Ur or Lagash, or mountain-kings of E'lam who conquered the land of Sumer.

But during this time of confusion, other Semitic tribes, Am'o-rites from Syria, had seized the town of Babylon, an obscure little backwoods village on the banks of the muddy Euphrates. Under the rule of these Amorite kings, Babylon grew in strength till at last she stood forth in splendor, the greatest of the cities of Sumer, greater than Sin and Larsa, grander than Ur and Nippur.

The Kings of Babylon conquered the last remaining descendant of the powerful Ur-En'gur of Ur and brought all Sumer and Akkad under the rule of Babylon. Then for the first time the Land of Two Rivers came to be called Babylonia.

Hammurabi, and the First Great Kingdom of Babylon
(2067 B.C. TO 2025 B.C.)

In those days, there came to the throne of Babylon, Hammu-ra'bi, the Mighty, the second great Semitic king. Still at heart half a herdsman, he loved his vast flocks of sheep

A group of Elamites from the mountain land that later became Persia, bowing to the ground for mercy before a King of Assyria. These mountaineers whom Hammurabi drove back to their hills were constantly swooping down on the plains and harrying Babylonia and Assyria. Note their plain short sleeved tunics, their bows and decorated quivers and the tasseled fillets on their heads. See the opposite page. (From an Assyrian Stone Carving.)

like his wandering Semitic ancestors; and he celebrated the sheep-shearing feast as his favorite festival. Yet he was a man of the city who spent long hours holding court or dictating brief clay letters to settle affairs of state.

Back to their mountain homes he drove the fierce tribes of Elam; he subdued the desert wanderers and held the restless cities of Sumer quiet beneath his rule. As'shur, Queen of Assyria, on her low bluff above the Tigris, Asshur he held in his hands; Babylon he fortified. Canals and reservoirs he dug; roads he laid; new shrines he built. All the gods of heaven, so his people said, rejoiced in Hammurabi, law-giver, warrior, builder.

When Hammurabi held court, great crowds thronged the passage-ways that led to the hall of state. In the midst of a bright-hued procession, preceded by men blowing trumpets, the Great King entered the hall, clad in his long, flowing garments, his square beard covering his breast, his upper lip clean-shaven after the desert custom. Behind him walked two attendants, one bearing the royal fly-whisk, the other

Hammurabi holds court. The figure of the lion-headed eagle holding two stags, was a copper relief found at Ur.

holding the long-handled royal umbrella over his head. Between rows of kneeling figures, the King advanced to the throne. Then courtiers began to chant:

"Hammurabi, glorious son of Sin'mu-bal'lit, came to his reign in the vigor of his youth. Out of our lands he drove the fierce tribes of Elam, back to their eastern mountains he sent them; tribes of the west to the desert he banished. Mighty in battle is Hammurabi! Roads to the cities, canals for the farmers, justice and prosperity for all peoples gave Hammurabi. Glorious in peace is he, chosen of Mar'duk!"

With a clash of cymbals the chant was ended, and the bearers of tribute came forward to lay gifts at the Great King's feet,—a casket of gold from Ninevah, stone figures of Ishtar from Sippar, and a silver girdle from Ur.

Next, there advanced post-runners, slim and muscular fellows, bringing the Great King messages from distant city governors, and after them, rows of petitioners whose cases Hammurabi patiently heard and judged.

Not till his long hours in court were over was the busy Hammurabi free to seek repose at last on the lofty roof of his palace which stood four stories high, rising up from a great mound of earth.

From his roof the King could see for miles over all the land around. To the west, across the Euphrates, sluggish and chocolate colored, he saw a flat green valley that melted in the distance into the purple haze. To the north and east and south, were vast rich stretches of green, that wonderland of fertility between the two great rivers. There grew corn and wheat, bearded barley, and vegetables, with cedar trees, cypress and palms.

Hammurabi receives from the sun-god the laws described on page 26. Rays are visible behind the shoulders of the sun-god. Hammurabi wears a turban and a long robe draped in long folds, with the right arm and shoulder bare. His upper lip is clean-shaven. (From the stele of Hammurabi recording the laws.)

Out from the city ran great stone roads, built by Hammurabi, and at intervals on all those roads, were well-kept postal stations, where relays of fresh runners stood ready to carry clay letters on a regular postal service between the different towns. Great caravans of merchants and those bring-

Unopened clay letters of Hammurabi's time. The king had a regular postal service between towns. The clay envelopes are addressed with the name of the person to whom the letter was sent and stamped with the seal impression of the sender. The envelopes at the right and left are broken at the top showing parts of the letters inside. (Yale Archaeological Collection.)

ing tribute to Babylon wound daily over these roads. And through all the fields and villages a network of canals stretched away from the river, providing a water supply that never failed through the year.

The Great King's heart was filled with pride. A rich land was that before him, a land second only to Egypt, where Am-en-em'het III now sat on the throne of the Pharaohs.

On the narrow, crooked streets of the royal city of Babylon, scores of little shops opened where each day people bargained for clothing, food and supplies. Soldiers were stationed at various points to keep the city in order, and the market square was crowded with caravans of asses loading and unloading their heavy bales of goods.

There, too, wild Kas'site mountaineers, a fierce white tribe from the eastern hills, brought a beautiful, strange, new animal which the people of Babylonia called the "beast of the mountains." This animal was the horse. The Kassites had got him in trade from the Indo-Europeans, the ancestors of the great white race, who then roved the

Kassite mountaineers, neighbors of the Elamites, show the first horses known in history to curious crowds in Babylon, about 2000 B.C. Heretofore the only beasts of burden known in Babylon had been the ox and the ass. These white-skinned highlanders, wild and barbarous men of the hills, later caused Babylon much trouble. Their beardless faces and costumes of turbans and short tunics are taken from Kassite seals, one of which is shown on page 289.

At the left a spinner of Hammurabi's day sits cross-legged on a stool while an attendant stands behind her with a fan. Her features are truly Semitic and she is a lady of high rank as her claw-legged furniture, her robe, and elaborate hair-dressing show. Before her on the table is a fish. (Carved stone from Susa; Paris, Louvre.) At the right are two boxers, a man with a kettledrum and a woman with castanets. (Babylonian Carvings, British Museum.)

Northern Grasslands beyond the Caspian Sea, catching the graceful wild horse as he raced and sniffed the wind in the freedom of the steppes.

Caravans from Si'nai and even from distant Egypt crossed the desert to Babylon, carrying stone and copper, silver, gold, and spices, to be exchanged for food. Cotton and teakwood came from India by boats on the Persian Gulf; cedarwood and marble were brought down from the hills.

Trade was the life of Babylon. In the crowded bazaars of the city the Semite merchants, in love with the noisy bustle of commerce, set up new standards of counting. They weighed things by the *mina*, which had the same weight as the pound; but they counted by sixties instead of tens,— 60 *shekels* to a *mina*, and 60 *minas* to a *talent**.

Moreover, as more and more trading was done, they discovered the use of money to take the place of barter. Silver was melted up and formed into pieces of different weights, so that when men spoke of a shekel, they meant a small bit of silver weighing one-sixtieth of a pound, and a talent was a large bar of silver weighing sixty pounds. Thus the Semites of Babylon invented the first form of money.

*It was from this method of counting that our hour was divided into 60 minutes and the minute into 60 seconds.

The temple of Marduk, the famous Tower of Ba'bel, at Babylon. This temple contained not only a ziggurat but business offices and storehouses. Poor peasants bearing a kid and a few palm branches stuck in a jar of water as an offering to the god, and priestesses in twisted robes and sacred crowns mingle among the merchants.

Commerce in Babylonia centered in the cities around the great, rambling temples. So rich grew these temples that they often loaned money to business men, and in Babylonia first arose the custom of charging interest, of giving drafts and receipts.

Even the priests grew interested in trade. In the very temples where priestesses sang fervent hymns to the "Father, long-suffering, and full of forgiveness," contracts were made, money was borrowed, slaves were hired, and goods were exchanged.

Babylon was indeed the "Great City, clothed in fine linen, and purple, and scarlet; decked with gold, and precious stones, and pearls; a city given to pleasures, that dwelt carelessly, whose merchants were the great men of the earth."

At last when Hammurabi had brought all Sumer and Akkad under his control, he ordered the Scribes to collect the various laws which he found in different parts of the land. He arranged these laws, made them over, and added others of his own. Then he ordered the new code carved on a pillar of the temple, while copies stamped on clay were sent to judges throughout the land.

This collection of Hammurabi's is the first known code of laws. It gave women almost the same rights as men and insisted on justice for all, but, strangely enough, it required that punishment for an injury should be in the form of the same injury to the person who had been guilty.

If a man had caused the loss of a gentleman's eye, his own eye must be put out. Thus the demand of "an eye for an eye, and a tooth for a tooth," which appears in the laws of Moses, began with Hammurabi.

The great Hammurabi, likewise, collected a library for his palace. In his day people learned to read and sent their children to schools very like our own schools of today.

The school house was a clay-brick building just inside the

A school in ancient Babylon 4000 years ago. The children squatting on mats on the floor are rocking back and forth and shouting their lessons aloud. Other children learn to write cuneiform letters by pressing the stylus into soft clay. Through the open door in the courtyard a child goes to the clay-box to get fresh clay for a tablet. The large tablet on the wall shows how picture signs for foot, horse, bird, and fish gradually changed to the wedge signs for the word. The signs at the right still bear some resemblance to the pictures at the left.

temple walls. There sat the school-master scribe waiting to greet the children within a very long room, on the walls of which hung tablets inscribed with the name of each child and a record of how many times he had been absent or tardy.

Beyond, in an open court from which opened other rooms, a box of soft clay stood ready to furnish the children material for making themselves new tablets.

In a separate room sat the younger children, making wedge shaped marks in the clay and painstakingly practicing writing, or copying ancient proverbs to guide their infant feet in the difficult paths of virtue.

> Thou shalt not slander—speak what is pure!
> Thou shalt not spread evil—speak kindly!
> Do not speak boastfully—guard thy lips;
> If in anger, do not speak out.

Other children, more advanced, were sent to the reading room where they had to memorize the meaning of more than 350 wedge groups and combinations!

Whole books they memorized aloud, dictionaries, readers, histories, geographies, and arithmetics. Squatting on mats on the ground, they rocked their bodies back and forth in a regular rhythm, each shouting his lesson shrilly and at the top of his lungs.

Girls were given the same education as boys in Babylonia and many women became scribes and clerks, stenographers and secretaries.

Thus under Hammurabi, Babylonia reached the height of her earlier development. His reign was the climax of a thousand years of progress in the Land of the Two Rivers. Schools, books and libraries offered to all opportunities for education; good government and freedom from war made manufacturing flourish; and trade and commerce were free to follow the well-guarded roads to every part of the land.

Weird demons: lion-headed monsters with legs like eagles, fight with daggers; the queer-looking scorpion-man shoots at a demon with human head on a lion's body; a horse-headed creature and a double-headed figure.

Beliefs Concerning Gods and Demons

The earliest Sumerians in the Land of the Two Rivers believed that a spirit lived in every object. Each tree, each stone, each pool, and spring contained a spirit or god.

The people believed also that certain demons or goblins wandered about the earth, and that these demons would attack and harm them unless they were controlled by magic charms or by prayers called incantations.

If a person was sick or suffering, jealous or in a rage, he was said to be possessed by devils who had entered his body by command of some god, or because of some magic spell cast by a sorcerer or a witch. Certain people called exorcists made a business of reciting incantations to drive these devils out. To the weird accompaniment of ghostly bluish fires made of fragrant herbs, the exorcist would dance and thus command the devils:

> "Away, away, far away, far away,
> Be ashamed, be ashamed! Fly, fly away!
> Turn about, go away, far away,
> Make your evil like the smoke mount to heaven!
> Out of my body away,
> Out of my body far away,
> Out of my body in shame,
> Out of my body fly away,
> Out of my body turn away,
> Out of my body go away.
> To my body do not return!"

A Sumerian worshipper conducted by two goddesses, one in a flounced robe, the other in a gown of long folds, approaches the bearded moon-god Sin, who sits on his throne with the symbol of his wife Nan'nar, goddess of the new moon just before him. A cylinder seal from the days of Hammurabi. The early Babylonian artists carved these seals with most delicate skill. They were usually little cylinders of stone which were rolled upon soft clay to leave raised impressions of the figures. Such seals were used for making signatures.

The most important gods in the land were the old nature gods of Sumer—Sha'mash, the sun-god; Sin, the moon-god; and A'nu, Lord of the Heavens.

Many of these had been tribal gods when the people lived in the mountains, and had become the special gods of the cities when the various tribes settled in the valley.

En-lil' of Nippur, was god of the wind; Bel and Ni'nib were war-gods. Mar'duk was a Semitic god, brought by the conquerors to Sumer; but he outranked Sumerian gods and became the chief god of Babylon. Some said he was the Creator.

Shamash, the sun-god of Sippar, sits upon a carved throne in his shrine, holding rod and ring, symbols of royalty or eternity. Above him are signs of the sun, the star Venus, and the moon. Before the shrine, the disk of the sun, supported by cords held by two lesser gods, stands upon an altar. A king is being led into the sun-god's presence by a priest and Aa, wife of the god. Relief from a temple at Babylon now in the British Museum.

How Marduk Created the World

In the beginning there was no earth, no sky. All was a watery chaos till Ap'su, the Deep, Mum'mu, the Water, and dread Ti-a'mat, the Sea, the lords of primeval chaos, created gods and monsters who floated on the teeming waters forever quarreling and striving amid the rage of billows.

Then the good gods chose E'a their leader and set themselves to bring about a reign of law and order. In the midst of primeval waters they waged a mighty conflict against the demons of Chaos. Apsu and Mummu they took captive; but Ti-a'mat raged the louder and gathered about her for a second battle all the monsters of the deep.

"Sharp of tooth and merciless of fang,
With poison instead of blood she filled their bodies;
She clothed with terror the terrible dragons,
Decking them with brilliancy, giving them a lofty stature . . .
She brought forth great serpents, dragons, and monsters,
Hurricanes, raging dogs, and scorpion-men;
Mighty tempests, fish men, and rams,
Bearing cruel weapons, fearless in combat,
Mighty in command, irresistible;
In all eleven monsters of this kind she made."

In the midst of primeval waters, Marduk fights Tiamat and her demons. See the demons, page 29; the combat, page 109.

So hideous was the aspect of all this frightful host, that no god dared to assail them, till Marduk rose up and agreed to give battle to dread Ti-a'mat. Loudly the gods rejoiced. To the feast-hall they summoned Marduk.

> Then they placed in their midst a garment,
> To test the power of Marduk, their first born. They said:
> "Thy fate, O Lord, be supreme among the gods!
> Declare that this garment vanish,
> And speak the word again that the garment reappear!"
> Then Marduk gave command, and the garment vanished;
> He commanded again, and the garment appeared.
> Then the gods, his fathers, thus beheld the power of his utter-
>   ance;
> They rejoiced and paid homage to Marduk, King;
> They bestowed on him scepter, throne and crown;
> They gave him dominion over all the gods.

So did Marduk go forth; to meet Ti-a'mat he went. His face he covered with the lightning; with burning flame his body he filled. Of the four winds he made a net to ensnare Tiamat, his foe; he sent before him the hurricane.

The leader of Tiamat's army, dazzled by the light that gleamed from Marduk's face, slunk away in despair, but Tiamat herself pressed forward with all her monstrous host.

On she came until Marduk halted her with a shout.

"Against the gods, my fathers, thou has planned evil," he cried. "Stand and let us join battle!"

> "Then stepped forth Ti-a'mat and Marduk leader of the gods.
> To fight they advanced, to battle they drew nigh.
> The lord spread his net and encompassed her,
> The storm-wind, stationed behind him, he drove in her face.
> Tiamat opened her mouth to its full extent.
> He drove in the storm-wind before she could close her lips.
> He overcame her and destroyed her life;
> He cast down her carcass and stood upon it."

Beholding their leader slain, the throng of Ti-a'mat was scattered; her host was broken up. But Marduk fell on the monsters; he took them captive and broke their weapons; he caught them in his net. They sat fast in his snare and filled the whole world with their wailings.

Then Marduk approached the body of Tiamat. He cut her in two like a fish. Of one half he made the earth; of the other half he made the sky and between he established the stations of all the stars. Nannar, the moon-god, he brought forth and entrusted with the night; he placed him to light the darkness and mark the passing of months.

Next, Marduk created mankind; he created the beasts of the field; he made all living things; Tigris and Euphrates he formed and he set them in their places; soil and grass, the marsh-plant, the reed, and the forest he planted.

The wild cow and her young, the wild ox, the ewe and her young, the lamb of the fold, the goat and the mountain goat he brought forth.

Houses and cities he made and temples for the gods.

Thus man dwelt on the earth and honored the gods on high.

So ended the story of Marduk, but since the people believed that the sun, the moon, and each of the stars was a god, set in place by Marduk, they thought that by watching the position of all these heavenly bodies, they could read the will of the gods and tell whether or not it was wise to undertake a journey, or embark on a business venture.

Babylon became a city of sorcerers, of diviners, astrologers, stargazers, and monthly prognosticators.

According to Babylonian views of the universe, the gods lived in the skies, men lived on earth, and in a dreary cave under the earth lived the unfortunate dead, inactive and neglected, feeding on dust and clay. Every year the god Tam'muz, husband of the earth-goddess Ish'tar, was ob-

Stargazers on a temple ziggurat. The priest measures the angles and movements of the stars with an astrolabe while his assistant draws a map of the heavens. Real knowledge of astronomy began in Babylon; but it was twisted to the uses of astrology, that the stargazers might foretell coming events. Sorcerers and diviners made prophecies from thunder-storms, earthquakes, eclipses and even by consulting clay-models of the liver of a sheep. See page 218.

liged to spend many months in the gloom of the Under-world. Then all the earth mourned for Tammuz; growth and fertility ceased and winter bound earth in chains.

The Story of Ishtar and Tammuz

Ishtar is the earth mother. At her command earth blooms and lambs and babes are born. But her love is a savage thing; in moments of rage she destroys the very things she has made. Beautiful is her face, hot her love, but terrible her fury.

Ishtar treading on a lion. Note her arrows, serpent wand, serpent sword and horned crown. From a Sumerian Seal 2000-1500 B.C.

Now it chanced that Ishtar loved Tammuz, the bright young god of the sun. And Ishtar wedded Tammuz, even as earth yields her riches to the wooing warmth of the sun. But Ishtar grew angry one day. In a fury she slew her young husband. The sun-god, beautiful, glowing, she sent to the dark Under-

world. Without him the earth grew cold, the earth grew
sad and dreary; all the earth mourned for Tammuz.

Then Ishtar repented her deed and she, too, wept for
Tammuz. She said: "I will go to the Underworld and bring
Tammuz back again."

Toward the Land of No-return, the region of darkness,
Ishtar, the daughter of the Moon-god, directed her way.
The Moon god's daughter directed her way to the house of
darkness, toward the house out of which he who enters,
never returns; toward the house where he who enters is
deprived of light; a place where dust is their sustenance, their
food clay; light they see not; they sit in darkness; they are
clothed like a bird with feathers.

At the gate of No-return, Ishtar cried out to the porter:
"Open thy gate lest I smash it!"

But the porter went within. To Al-la'tu, Queen of the
Underworld, he announced the coming of Ishtar.

Like a broken ku-ne'nu reed, Al-la'tu sank together.

"Admit her," she cried; "but disrobe her according to
ancient law."

The porter opened to Ishtar; at the first gate he took off

Ishtar, beautiful but terrible, storms the gates of the Underworld. To the Babylonians, seeing only a material
cause in the life of the universe, Ishtar, the earth-mother created living things only to make them decay and die.
Ishtar was variously called Ash'to-reth or As-tar'te in the lands of Syria, Palestine and the West. See page 241.

her crown; at the second gate, her earrings; at the third, her jeweled necklace; at the fourth, her gleaming breast ornaments; at the fifth, her enameled belt; at the sixth, her bracelets and anklets; and at the seventh, her loin cloth, her last remaining garment.

So Ishtar stood naked and shivering before the dark Queen of the Dead. And with each advancing step of Ishtar's enforced disrobing, vegetation withered on earth. The world, like Ishtar, stood naked; the world stood naked like Ishtar, naked, forlorn and shivering.

Ishtar took no counsel; she threw herself on Al-la'tu; Allatu, in anger, smote her, smote her with sore disease. On earth all nature seemed perishing, lifeless, and withered as Ishtar.

Then Ea, King of the Universe, decided to rescue Ishtar and grant her the life of Tammuz. He made a mortal man, to bear his commands to Allatu. And Allatu smote her sides; she cursed the unfortunate mortal. Nevertheless, she was forced to restore health to Ishtar's limbs, to let her go forth in safety.

Once more the porter led Ishtar out through the seven gates. At each gate he restored unto her the ornaments which he had taken; and with each bright jewel returned, the earth above woke up, gradually blooming again and covering herself, like Ishtar, with her jewels of grass and flowers.

At the last gate Tammuz appeared and was restored to Ishtar, clad in fine raiment and linen, and piping upon his flute. The lovers embraced with rapture, and as they stepped forth from Underworld gloom, they emerged into brilliant sunlight; on earth all was summer once more.

Nevertheless, each year Tammuz must go again to the gloom of the Underworld, to remain there with Allatu or to go as porter to the gates of heaven, and while he is absent, winter reigns and all the earth mourns for Tammuz; but when he returns, earth rejoices and summer comes back again.

The south-wind overturns Adapa's boat. The longing for eternal life, deep-rooted in the heart of the Babylonians, finds tragic expression in their folk tales like this one of Adapa, and the Epic of Gilgamesh. The hopelessness of their faith; their belief in a gloomy, terrible, existence after death, made every such tale end with the loss of eternal life. Some scholars see in this story a likeness to the Bible tale of how Adam lost eternal life.

The Story of Adapa and the South Wind

Often mortals longed to escape the gloom of the Underworld and find eternal life, but they could never accomplish it. The gods would not have it so. Even Ea, the kindly father of mankind, deceived his son, A'da-pa, into refusing immortal life at the moment when he had grasped it.

Ea created Adapa to be his own son. He bestowed upon him wisdom, prudence, an intelligent mind; but he did not give him eternal life. Now Adapa dwelt as a fisherman by the seaside. One day he steered his boat into the wide lagoon when the South Wind blew up a storm. Like a bird of ill-omen she came; she ducked the fisherman under; to the dwelling of the fishes she made him sink. Thereupon Adapa cried: "O South Wind, thou hast made me swallow thy foam as much as thou darest! I will break thy wing!"

And Adapa brake her wing; for seven days the South Wind could not rage over the land, nor sweep the sea with her storm wings. Then Anu, god of the heavens, rose in a rage from his throne crying: "Bring me hither this Adapa who hath insulted the gods!"

And Adapa, thus summoned, set forth to climb up to heaven; but Ea his creator, gave him a word of counsel:

"Behold, this is time of winter and Tammuz, the bright young sun-god, is absent from the earth, standing porter at heaven's gate. Do thou put on garments of mourning, and when thou art come to Tammuz, win his goodwill by saying: 'I mourn for the absence of Tammuz.' Then will Tammuz intercede for thee before the high face of Anu. Nevertheless," said Ea, "drink not of the drink; eat not of the food which they in heaven will offer thee; food and drink of death is that which they set before thee."

Thereafter Adapa did as Ea had commanded him. He clad himself in mourning garments. He climbed to heaven. He won the goodwill of Tammuz and of his comrade, Gish-zi'da, who stood at the gate of heaven.

And Tammuz and Gishzida pacified Anu's anger. Anu grew calm again as a sea when the wind has subsided.

And Anu said: "Now hath a mortal man climbed up to us in heaven. What shall we do for him? We must even make him immortal, one of ourselves; for it is not meet that a mortal should know the secrets of the gods. Bring bread of life that he may eat of it and water of life, that he may drink of it."

But Adapa touched not the bread. Adapa drank not the water. Adapa hearkened to Ea's words, Ea's false words of counsel; he thought what was set before him was water and bread of death; it was water and bread of life. So was Adapa tricked; so he refused immortality; he went back to earth still a mortal, and so did mortal man lose eternal life.

The Story of Etana and His Flight to Heaven

E-ta'na, another hero, likewise sought to reach Anu's heaven; for the eagle said to Etana; "My friend, let me carry thee upward unto the heaven of Anu. On my breast place thy breast; on my pinions place thy hands."

So Etana mounted the eagle and they rose in daring flight for the space of a double hour.
"Look, my friend," said the eagle. "The earth appears as a mountain, the sea has become a pool."
For a second double hour the

Etana, at the right, mounts to heaven clinging with one arm to the neck of the eagle. The moon is just above him. Below, two barking dogs, a man with something like an umbrella, a goatherd and even his three goats, all look up in amazement at Etana's flight. Over the goatherd a potter makes jars and at the right of the jars a squatting baker makes round loaves. The drawing is from an impression made upon clay by a bronze cylinder seal.

eagle carried Etana; the eagle carried Etana for a second double hour. Onward they flew and upward.

"Look, my friend," said the eagle; "the sea is now a mere belt that girdles the little earth."

A third double hour they flew, till they came to the heavenly gate, and there they alighted to rest.

But the eagle urged Etana to mount up higher still, to mount to the realms of Ishtar, Princess among the gods.

Once more for three double hours they took their flight onward and upward; the sea seemed a little courtyard, the earth a garden-bed.

Then Etana begged the eagle to cease his daring flight.

But, alas, they had flown too high; already they had flown too high. Ishtar, the terrible, spied them, saw them mounting the heavens, the dwelling place of the gods. Like lightning, she hurled them to earth; she flung them down whence they came.

The eagle was stripped of his feathers, and Etana was sent in disgrace to the gloom of the Underworld.

Gil'ga-mesh knew of their fate; yet did this third hero, Gilgamesh, dare to search heaven's secrets and seek eternal life.

The wild man, Eabani, half-bull, half-beast, is led by the woman to see that he is more than a beast, that he is like to a god. She leads him away from the beasts, out of the jungle to the city, the next step in civilization.

The Story of the Strong Man, Gilgamesh*

In walled E'rech, the ancient, men wept and women sighed; for one laid siege to the city,—Gil'ga-mesh, the Kassite, irresistible in power, like to a mountain-bull, surpassing men in strength. And Gilgamesh took the city; he triumphed over the warriors. He snatched the sons from their fathers, the virgins from their mothers.

Then did the people of Erech cry to the goddess Ar'u-ru, that she might create a man to stand against this Gilgamesh.

Aru-ru washed her hands; she took a piece of clay; she threw the clay on the ground and lo, she created Ea-ba'ni.

A wild man was Eabani; his body was covered with hair; among beasts of the forest he dwelt; he ate herbs with the gazelles; he drank from a trough with the cattle; he sported with the creatures of the waters.

Now Gilgamesh sent a hunter to snare the savage wildman; but the hunter could not catch him. So Gilgamesh bade the hunter take the beautiful woman Ukh'a-tu to charm the dreaded Eabani.

And Eabani loved the woman; and the woman said to Eabani: "Lofty art thou, Eabani, like to a god. Why dost thou dwell with the beasts? Come with me to walled Erech."

*The epic of Gilgamesh is the finest piece of Babylonian literature remaining to us today. Gilgamesh was a real Kassite leader whose deeds were so enlarged and interwoven with myth as to lose all semblance of history. The story was found on 12 separate clay tablets. It spread from Babylon to all lands, influencing the Greek story of the strong man Hercules and the Bible stories of Samson and of the Flood.

Eabani left the gazelles; Eabani took leave of the oxen; Eabani clave to the woman. The woman became his companion; she led him out of the jungle back to the city of Erech; they put on festival garments with them who kept holiday.

But soon there came against Erech, out of the mountains of Elam, Khum-ba′ba, the terrible one, horribly threatening Erech. Before him men bowed in terror as before the rage of the storm-wind.

Then Gilgamesh said to Eabani: "Come and join friendship with me. On a great couch I will place thee. Rulers of the earth shall kiss thy feet, if thou wilt go with me to fight against this Khumbaba."

Eabani swore friendship to Gilgamesh. Together they travelled the road. Together they saw before them a grove of wonderful grandeur, in the midst of which a cedar tree gave shade and diffused sweet odor.

There stood Khumbaba's fortress. The comrades fell on the tyrant and Gilgamesh battled and slew him.

Gilgamesh slew Khumbaba; and, rising up as a victor, he took off his blood-stained garments; he robed himself in pure white; he placed a crown on his head.

Thus did great Ishtar behold him. Ishtar, Queen of the gods, mistress of destruction, she who unchains the

Ishtar the goddess, offers the hero Gilgamesh a chariot of lapis-lazuli and gold if he will become her husband.

terrors of war, she looked on the victor and loved him.

And Ishtar said unto Gilgamesh: "Be thou my husband; I will give thee a chariot of lapis-lazuli and gold, with wheels of gold and horns of sapphire. Thou shalt dwell in a sweet-smelling house of cedar. Kings, lords, and princes shall bring thee tribute!"

But Gilgamesh knew well the furious cruelty of Ishtar and how she had once slain Tammuz and plucked the beautiful feathers of the bright al-lal'lu bird. So he refused to wed her.

Then Ishtar flew in a rage and mounted up to Anu, to Anu, lord of the heavens. She uttered loud complaints against the hero, Gilgamesh.

To comfort the goddess Ishtar, Anu created a bull; Anu made Alu, the strong one; Anu sent forth the bull, snorting with rage of destruction, that he might destroy the hero.

But Gilgamesh and Eabani went forth against the monster. Eabani seized its tail; Gilgamesh lifted his spear; he pierced the great beast to its heart. Loud rose rejoicings in Erech.

Violent as destruction, Ishtar climbed to the wall, the outer wall of walled Erech, and she hurled forth hideous curses against the hero, Gilgamesh. But Eabani flung full in her face the carcass of the dead bull.

"I will do to thee," he shouted, "as I have done to this bull!"

Gilgamesh fights the bull, aided by his friend Eabani. A fine old Babylonian seal of the time of Sargon I.

Then Ishtar, in terrible silence, caused Eabani to die; and she sent disease upon Gilgamesh, till all his strength was gone and he, too, was like to die. Sadly he mourned for Eabani, mourned for the loss of his comrade. Sadly he wandered with slow-dragging feet, suffering and seeking healing, longing to learn how mortal man might make himself immortal.

At length the hero bethought him of the one and only mortal who had ever escaped from death, Ut-na-pish'-tim, the distant one, who lived far off and far off, at the Meeting-Place-of-the-Streams. The road there was full of dangers. The road there was full of terrors.

Gilgamesh traveled the road, traveled through dan-

Gilgamesh and the lion. A masterpiece of Sumerian art.

gers and terrors. He came to a glen at nightfall. Lions he saw and was frighted. He raised his head in the dark and prayed unto Sin, the moon-god. He fought with and strangled a lion.

Then passed he out of the glen and came to the mountain, Nash'u. From sunrise to sunset the mountain reached and, within, it went down unto Ar'a-lu, the dust-covered cave of the dead. Scorpion-men guarded its gate, of terror-inspiring aspect, whose appearance was deadly.

With awful words they described the dangers of that dread district to which Gilgamesh sought an entrance; yet Gilgamesh persisted; the Scorpion-men opened the gate; the hero entered the mountain.

For one double hour Gilgamesh groped his way in dense darkness; for two double hours Gilgamesh groped his way in dense darkness; but after twelve double hours he beheld before him a tree, a tree of splendid appearance, whose fruit was precious stones.

Then came he to the sea, the waters whereof surround

Gilgamesh beseeches the maiden Sabitum to let him pass over the sea in his search for the secret of eternal life.

the earth and flow under it, the sea on the banks of which the maiden Sab'i-tum dwells in her palace and on her throne.

Beholding the hero coming, the maiden locked her gates.

"Thou shalt not pass through," she said. "Thou shalt not pass over this sea."

Then Gilgamesh pleaded with Sabitum; he told of Eaba-ni's death and how he came seeking the secret which should save him forever from dying. The maiden only replied:

"No one hath crossed this ocean. Difficult is the passage. Impassable are the Waters of Death that are guarded by a bolt. There is but one chance of thy crossing. Seek out Ar'di E'a, ferryman of Ut-na-pish'tim. If he will take thee across, all is well; if not, then thy hope must die."

So Gilgamesh sought Ardi Ea. The ferryman heard his plea and promised to take him the journey.

A huge pole did Gilgamesh cut, a stout pole to serve as a rudder. They two entered into the vessel.

The ship tossed to and fro; for a month and fifteen days the ship tossed about in the waters.

Then came they unto swift rapids, wild, savage, dark, foaming waters, the dangerous Waters of Death.

"Hold fast," Ardi Ea shouted. "Hold thou fast to the rudder!"

Strong was the powerful current, strong to bear them away; but Gilgamesh clung to the rudder.

Utnapishtim astonished on the shore, perceives Gilgamesh and Ardi Ea crossing the dangerous Waters of Death.

They passed through the Waters of Death; they passed the dark waters in safety; and there on the shore they beheld him, Ut-na-pish′tim himself, astonished to see a mortal man approaching across those wild rapids.

From the vessel the hero addressed him, recounting the death of Eabani, and begging to know by what means he himself might escape from the fate of dying.

"No mortal man may escape from death," Utnapishtim made answer.

"Then how is it thou hast escaped?" Gilgamesh flung back the question.

"Come hither and I will tell thee," Utnapishtim replied; and as Gilgamesh sought the shore and seated himself on the bank, Utnapishtim told Gilgamesh the *Story of the Flood*.

Thus spake the great Ut-na-pish′tim:

"The city of Shu′rip-pak did evil; the gods said: 'Let us destroy it.'

Bel, the warrior, Ni′nib, dread bearer of destruction, Anu, Lord of the Heavens, and Ea, Father of Waters, agreed to destroy the city by means of a terrible rain storm.

"Yet the heart of Ea yearned toward mankind. He could not forbear a warning; and to me he appeared in a dream, saying: 'The Lord of the Whirlstorm will cause destruction to rain upon thee in the evening. Therefore build thee a ship. Make the house thereof 120 cubits wide and as many cubits high. Six stories, one above another, shalt thou build. Then take thy family into the ship and take, likewise, every kind of living beast."

"So I did as Ea commanded. I built a flat bottomed skiff. I built it with upturned edges. On it I placed a house, a dwelling place of six stories. I caused to enter the ship my family, and my household, with all kinds of living beasts.

Then I looked at the sky; I was terrified, and I, too, entered the vessel. Behind me, I closed the door.

"In the sky dark clouds appeared, within which the Lord of the Whirlstorm caused his thunder to roll.

Over mountain and land the destroyers passed; Dib'ba-ra, lord of pestilence, let loose the forces of mischief; Ninib, the terrible one, advanced in a fury of hate.

The An-nu-na'ki, spirits, lords of the dreaded lightning, raised aloft their torches; their sheen illumined the sky.

As Ram'man's whirlwind swept by, all light was changed to darkness. Terror fell upon gods and men. Brother cared not for brother; each man cared but for himself. The gods ran to seek a refuge in the midst of the highest heavens. Like dogs, they cowered in the sky.

Having let loose the lords of destruction, the gods could not now control them. They had meant to destroy only Shur'ip-pak. Behold, they destroyed the whole earth!

"Ishtar, the earth-mother, groaned; and gods and spirits wept with her. They sat overwhelmed with grief.

For six days and nights the hurricane waged war like the noise of an host; but when the seventh day dawned, rain ceased, and the sea became calm.

Bitterly weeping, I looked from the ship. All mankind was returned to clay. In every direction round about, I could see nothing save water.

Then the ship approached Mt. Ni'sir and clung to the peak of the mount. For six days the vessel hung there;

but when the seventh day dawned, I sent forth a dove to see if the waters had somewhat abated.

The dove flew round about but, finding no resting place, returned again to the ship.

Then I sent forth a swallow. The swallow flew round about, but finding no resting place, returned again to the ship.

Then I sent forth a raven. The raven flew off and found mud in which it cautiously waded. It came no more to the ship.

"So was I satisfied that the waters at last had subsided. I left the ship; I offered up sacrifice; on the top of the mountain I sacrificed to the gods. In seven bowls I placed calamus, cedar-wood and incense. The gods inhaled the odor. The gods inhaled the sweet odor; like flies they gathered together around the sacrifice. Ishtar swore by her necklace never to forget that day nor to let the floods loose again. Bel alone was enraged; all mankind he desired to destroy; he was angry at my escape. Then said Ea to Bel: 'Punish the sinner for his sins. Punish the evil-doer for his evil deeds, but do not root out all men. Show thy mercy to some.'

"At his words Bel repented. Bel entered into the ship; he took me by the hand; he caused my wife to kneel by my side; he stepped between us to bless us; he said: 'Hitherto Utna-pishtim has been mortal, but now shall he and his wife be immortal like to the gods.'

"So the gods took me and placed me to dwell at the Meeting-Place-of-the-Streams. So I became immortal; but this gift of eternal life is for no other mortal man. Thee I can heal of disease, but unless thou canst find the plant called 'Restoration-of-Old-Age-to-Youth,' thou canst not escape from dying."

There fell a deep sleep on Gilgamesh. The wife of Utna-pishtim brewed a magic drink and gave it to the sleeping hero. Refreshed, he awoke from his slumber and Ardi Ea bore him off to bathe in the fountain of life. Therein he disported his limbs and he came forth healed of his sickness.

In good health and strength again, he set forth to find that precious plant, "Restoration-of-Old-Age-to-Youth."

He came at last to a fountain. He saw the flower at the bottom gleaming amid the pure water. He stretched forth his hand; he seized it; he had it fast in his grasp. He went to pull it forth, when lo, a serpent rose up and snatched the plant from his fingers. Eternal life was lost. It was lost to him now forever.

Gilgamesh sat down and wept. He poured out his woe to the ferryman; but there was naught to do now. He must return to Erech and live the life of a mortal.

In safety he came to Erech. A hero he lived till he died.

II

The Assyrian Empire

Kassites, Mitannians, and Hittites in Asia Minor

(1600 B.C. TO 1100 B.C.)

When Hammurabi died, the power of Babylon soon passed; for Sam'su-i-lu'na, the great king's son, was by no means as strong as his father. Reports of the bountiful golden crops, and of the ease and prosperity enjoyed in the Plain of Shinar, were carried up into the rugged hills where dwelt the fierce Kassite horse breeders. Tempted by these reports, the bold mountaineers came down to make raids on the valley.

A Kassite mountaineer in short tunic and turban. From a Kassite seal.

Like swift birds of prey they descended, ravaging fields and villages, seizing grain, flocks, and herds, and stealing the treasures of the temples. And woe to the caravans from the east which must pass through the narrow defiles of the Kassite mountain-land. The savage, pale-faced mountaineers robbed and pillaged and murdered.

At last they overran and conquered all Babylonia; and their rule put an end to the progress of Semite-Sumerian days; for the only gift to civilization made by these mountaineers was spreading the use of the horse.

Assyria broke away and gained her independence; and henceforth for ten long centuries Babylonia counted little in the history of the world.

To the north of the Plain of Shinar in the great bend of the Upper-Euphrates, dwelt the prosperous, white-skinned Mi-tan'ni, lords of much fertile grain-land, intelligent, active folk, who had built up one of the strongest kingdoms in the

49

Teshub, the Hittite weather-god, bearing the forked lightning. Note his tall peaked hat, his pigtail and characteristic Hittite boots with upturned toes (see 97, 104-5, Vol. I, 228). Next, Teshub stands on a bull whose bellow
is the thunder. A priest-king pours a libation and a boy brings a goat for an offering. Modern excavations at Carchemish and the more ancient Hittite capital, Boghaz Keui, are revealing many interesting facts about the Hittites.

land. To the west of Mitanni were the Hit'tites, that curious
mixture of races, who made their weapons of iron and wore
pigtails like the Chinese.

Thus, in the year 1600 B.C., there were in the Land of Two
Rivers, the two small kingdoms of Assyria and Babylonia,
with endless unconquered highland-tribes in the mountains
to the east, and threatening them to the northward, the
Hittites of the iron mines and the Mitanni of the plains.

Into this welter of hostile tribes came Egypt in her days of

Little Hittite children playing knuckle bones and whip-top. Nearby a nurse carries a baby and leads the children's
pet. Reliefs from the later Hittite capital Car'che-mish.

Attendants of the Mi-tan′ni-an Princess, Tadukhipa, wife of Am-en-ho′tep IV, in the royal harem at El Amarna. These white skinned Mitannian maidens wear their hair divided into separate tresses curled at the end, a custom very different from Egyptian wigs. At the left a woman teaches two girls to play a duet on a lyre and a lute. Next another woman plays for the dance of two Mitannian girls who wear the flounced Asiatic robe. See Vol. I, p. 97.

power. Up through Canaan and Syria marched the sturdy old Thut′mose I, and his grandson Thutmose III, who conquered the Mitanni and took tribute even of Assyria.

While Egypt held control, there was an end of fighting. Richly laden caravans went safely from Memphis to Babylon, and merchants from many different lands camped peacefully side by side beneath the desert stars.

The Pharaohs took wives from Asia; Thutmose IV, Amenhotep III, and Amenhotep IV all married Mitannian princesses; friendship arose between nations; international laws began.

Then came Ram′ses II and broke the Hittite power, so that, in the later days, when cruel strife and disunion weakened the hands of Egypt, Assyria had no rival left in all the vast stretch of Asia.

The little state on the Tigris was free at last to expand. True, she was as yet nothing; she owned some eighty square miles of unirrigated plains and barren rocky hills; but she was a nation of warriors, pitiless and cruel; her kings had a mighty ambition and for generations they fought to make their little kingdom the greatest power in the world.

Tiglath Pileser I, and the Rise of Assyria

(1100 B.C. TO 1070 B.C.)

No more was Egypt the Queen of the world; the Hittite Empire had split up into numberless petty kingdoms; the white-skinned Mitanni were gone; Sea peoples from the Ae-ge'an Isles had settled the coast of Phi-lis'ti-a; Hebrews were seizing Ca'naan; wandering Ar'a-mae'an, another Semitic tribe from the vast Arabian Desert, strong, intelligent men, were swarming into Syria. In the mountains of Ar-me'-ni-a and Persia dwelt a hopeless confusion of native tribes, seething in constant unrest, but with no sort of organization.

Such was the world when Tig'lath Pi-le'ser I came to the throne of Assyria and set forth, bent on conquest, eleven hundred years before Christ.

The bodies of his enemies, like the storm-god, he hurled to the earth. Their blood in the ravines and on the heights of the mountains he made to flow down. Their heads he cut off; by the side of their cities, like grain heaps, he piled them up.

By difficult trails and steep passes which no former king had passed through, he crossed sixteen mighty mountains. In smooth and open country he marched with his chariots; in the wild and tangled uplands he opened a way with axes.

Crossing the Euphrates, he fell upon twenty-three allied kings, whom he conquered and forced to pay tribute.

Then, turning about to the southward, he defeated the King of Babylon; he burned his splendid palaces; he seized his land and cities.

At length, to crown his deeds, Tiglath Pileser swept through Syria to the sea, the first of Assyrian monarchs to look on the Med-i-ter-ra'nean, the Sea of the Setting Sun.

Men of Ar'vad, an island city, gave him a ride in their ships and helped him to kill a great whale, the spouting "horse of the sea." Byb'lus and Si'don, two rich Phoenician

An Assyrian camp. The circular stone outer wall with its battlements is divided by two streets at right angles. Within men are preparing food. At the entrance of the royal pavilion an official receives a group of bound captives driven by a soldier with a mace. Before the pavilion horses are being fed and groomed, and in the upper right corner two clowns in lion-skins dance to the music of a guitar. From the palace of Ashur-nasir-apal.

cities, hastened to send him tribute, as did the Great King of the Hittites.

Even Nes-u-ba-neb'ded, King of Lower Egypt, sent him a crocodile, in weak reversal of that proud day when a terrified King of Assyria had humbly sent his gifts to Thutmose the Great, of Egypt.

But while Tiglath Pileser disported himself hunting whales in the sea, swarms of Aramaeans, poured across the Euphrates and threatened to cut off the pass by which he must return home. Henceforth, these Aramaeans became his foremost foes. Month after month and year after year he turned this way and that to attack them, even in glaring midsummer when the dry and barren steppes burned and glowed with heat as from the fires of a furnace.

Tiglath Pileser, the burning flame, the terrible one, the storm of battle, was the first Assyrian King to organize conquered princes into a sort of Empire, to overwhelm many lands with the splendor of his majesty, and to call himself: "King of all princes, lord of lords, mighty one, King of the four quarters of the earth, King of the Universe."

Tiglath Pileser I forces his way to the Mediterranean, and Egypt, once so mighty, bows before the rising power of Assyria. Nesubenebded, King of Lower Egypt, sends a crocodile to Tiglath Pileser. For the weakened power of Egypt in Syria at this time see "The Misfortunes of Wenamon," Vol. I, p. 237. See also map, p. 70.

The glories of his reign, however, vanished with Tiglath Pileser. Under twelve weak successors, Assyria shrank up again and lost her neighboring possessions.

The Aramaeans advanced. In Syria they had already built large and splendid cities with handsome, well-furnished palaces. Their merchants, with long caravans, were now traveling everywhere, controlling the trade by land, just as the great Phoenician cities, after the downfall of Egypt, were controlling the trade by sea.

These Aramaeam merchants gave bills and receipts which

were written on paper with ink, and so displaced the earlier cuneiform tablet receipts given by traders from Babylon.

Moreover, through these business documents they spread from Persia to India and west to the Mediterranean, the Ar-a-ma'ic alphabet which they had borrowed from the Phoenicians. Their language, called Ar-a-ma'ic, was speedily becoming the general language of trade, and they were already exercising that deep influence on civilization which was to continue for ages. So far were they penetrating into Mes'o-po-ta'mi-a that they constantly rivaled Assyria.

Ashur-nazir-apal and his Deeds of Terror

(885 B.C. TO 860 B.C.)

It was not till two hundred years after Tiglath Pileser I, that there came to the throne in Assyria a man determined to face these swarms of Ara-maeans, A'shur-na'zir-apal' II, a king as cruel and warlike as Tiglath Pileser I, and one who aimed to domineer over all the surrounding tribes, thinking to terrify them by the frightfulness of his deeds.

He set out on his conquests accompanied by his army which consisted of slingers and bowmen, chariots and men on horseback, with the dreaded Assyrian invention, the infernal battering ram.

Sculptured relief of Ashur-nazir-apal, showing the king wearing the royal cap and grasping the staff of royalty. His fringed garment is covered with elaborate embroidery. This relief is in the British Museum.

Assyrians on horseback slaughter Aramaean foes while a bird of prey lingers above to devour the dead. One fallen Aramaean has already lost his head and a horseman just passing him appears to have attached the head to his horse's chest. These Semitic Aramaeans, distant cousins of the Hebrews, were settling many scattered kingdoms in Syria and becoming Assyria's most powerful foes. Some, as Egyptian wall-paintings show, had shock-heads of bushy red hair. Others had black hair and round pointed beards. Their warriors wear simple short tunics and a fillet around the head. (From the palace of Ashur-nazir-apal.)

In the hill-country to the east, he penetrated steep mountains which rose like the point of a dagger. Strongholds on breathless heights, like the nest of the vulture, he conquered. Wherever a fortress hung in the sky like to a cloud from heaven, his warriors flew like birds and conquered the nest on the rocks.

And from the difficult hill-country, the King turned back to the plains, to punish Aramaean rebels on the beautiful strip of green meadow-land along the river Habur. The miserable chief of the rebels he calmly ordered flayed.

Ashur-nazir-apal returns home in triumph while his god Ashur hovers above. (Cast in Metropolitan Museum, N.Y.)

"I erected a pillar opposite his city gate," the young King said, with cool delight in reciting the list of his tortures. "All the chiefs who had revolted, I flayed. With their skins I covered the pillar; some in the midst I walled up."

So Ashur-nazir-apal went his way of destruction, leaving behind him a trail of hands and noses and ears cut off, eyes put out, and pyramids of living piled beside heaps of severed heads.

One rebellious prince, named Sha'da-du, hard-pressed by the Assyrians, plunged into the river Euphrates to escape this terrible foe. Not waiting to take off his cloak, he seized a goat skin to float on, and madly threw himself into the stream, puffing away at the opening to blow up the skin as he swam. Behind him came his son and a wounded warrior, swimming.

From the towers of a town on the shore, two women and an anxious old man watched the escape of the fugitives, while Assyrian archers shot at them from among the palms and olive-trees along the river bluffs. In spite of their foes however, Shadadu and his son escaped to the further bank.

The rebellious prince, Shadadu and his son escape across the Euphrates on inflated skins. They have leapt into the water in such mad haste that they blow up the skins as they float. Foes shoot at them from the shore.

At length in the year 877 B.C., Ashur-nazir-apal himself, crossed the river Euphrates, sitting upright and stern in his chariot, which was borne along on a raft afloat on inflated skins. Syria was in tumult at news of the approach of this terrible Assyrian. Hittite states and Phoenician cities hastened to send him tribute.

Like the mighty Tiglath Pileser I, he pushed through to the Mediterranean, and collected a curious menagerie offered to him in tribute,—fifty powerful lions from the mountains; fifty cubs for cages in Assyrian palaces; a great and little dolphin; wild bulls, elephants, partridges, asses, gazelles, and panthers.

With all his wars, however, the amount of land really gained by Ashur-nazir-apal was most surprisingly small. The important thing that he did was to stem the fast advancing tide of Aramaean settlement, so these strong and intelligent Semites crowded no nearer Assyria.

In the last days of his reign, Assyria was at peace; Assyrian artists did great work and for the first time their bas-reliefs recorded the doings of history, showing Shadadu in his flight or Ashur-nazir-apal himself beneath his great state umbrella, beginning the siege of a city.

Shalmaneser III, and His Successors
(860 B.C. TO 722 B.C.)

With the death of Ashur-nazir-apal, his son, Shal-ma-ne'-ser III, came to the throne of Assyria.

The new king was no less fond of frightfulness than his father; and no less anxious to tyrannize over surrounding nations.

"Strong hero," he called himself; "who in the four quarters of the world gives no pardon; who conquers rebellion; who is covered with splendor."

Nevertheless, in spite of all these powerful titles, Shalmaneser could not escape a certain weakness of temper. He posed in splendid robes before admiring throngs, but he was not a stern, overbearing force like Ashur-nazir-apal.

In his days, Babylon was too strong to be attacked as yet, the Aramaean advance was checked, and the medley of Medean tribes in the difficult hills to the east were too unorganized to threaten any danger. So Shalmaneser cast greedy eyes on the far off cities of Syria,—they offered such wealth of booty at such a very small cost, they had so little unity, they constantly fought each other, and Egypt was too weak to give them any aid.

The brief and glorious Hebrew kingdom of the days of David and Solomon had broken up into the two petty nations known as Judah and Israel; and north of them in Syria was the Aramaean kingdom of Sa'mal, the Hittite kingdom of Ha'math, and many other little kingdoms, far too numerous to name.

But, unfortunately for Shalmaneser, a powerful enemy had grown up in the northern hills of Armenia. This country, called U-rar'tu by the Assyrians, was the Ar'a-rat

Two ambassadors from the king of Armenia are shown how the Assyrians torture their enemies, striking them over the head with a mace or flaying them. The Armenians, also known as Haldians, are the two figures at the left wearing elaborate turbans. From a relief in the British Museum.

Men impaled on stakes and pillars of heads before an Armenian city. Little Haldians fight with Assyrians; others in crested helmets and shoes, are driven off as prisoners. Separate figures from the gates of Shalmaneser.

of the Bible; its people were the stout, little Hal'di-ans, and their threat in the north was so powerful that Shalmaneser had to deal with them before he dared go into Syria.

Over hills which reached to heaven, he hewed a way for his chariots and reached the border of Haldia at the fortress of Su-ga'ni-a, which stood perched high on a rock. The little

Assyrian chariots and horses are led with great difficulty over the high rocky hills of Armenia which are represented as always in Assyrian sculpture, by pyramids of round stones. Below, Assyrian archers, clad in mail and each protected by a shield-bearer, storm the city of Sugania which has already burst into flames. The beautiful bands of hammered bronze from which these pictures were taken covered wooden gates 20 feet high, which stood at the entrance of the palace of Shalmaneser. The rosettes of beaded circles surround each nail head. (British Museum.)

Shalmaneser celebrates his victory on the shores of Lake Van. In the center of the picture, an image of the king has been carved on the rock of a hill side. Nearby one man throws the leg and another the head of a sacrificed ox into the lake. Monsters of the deep devour the sacrifice. Before the King's image are two royal standards, a table for offerings, a tall incense burner and a libation jar on an ox-footed support. The King pours out a libation.

Haldians, naked, yet wearing crested helmets, made desperate resistance; but their fortress fell, their houses were burned, men were impaled on stakes, severed heads were hung at the gates, and the smoke and flames of fourteen villages, fired by the Assyrians, leapt fiercely into the sky.

Without meeting further resistance, Shalmaneser pressed on to Lake Van, where he celebrated his victory beneath the lofty mountains that range the curving shore. Marching on foot in triumphal procession, preceded by the royal standards and followed by high officials and musicians playing their harps, he advanced to the shore of the lake and offered bulls and rams in sacrifice to the gods.

Yet the damage Shalmaneser had done on this swift raid to the northward, affected only one small part of his plucky rival Haldia. A-ra-me', the King of the land, had not been engaged in the struggle. The next spring, as soon as the snow had melted in the high-lying mountain passes, Shalmaneser set forth again. Through wild trails and pathless uplands, he reached the source of the Tigris, where amid savage scenery and the wildest of savage tribes, the full-grown river emerged from a cave, to flow through the depths of a rocky gorge on its way to the distant plains. From here Shalmaneser pressed on to Armenia's capital city.

Again the little Haldians, armed with swords and javelins, and now wearing short skirts and shoes, put up a plucky resistance, even seizing the bridles of the horses in a vain attempt to stay the Assyrian advance.

The mounted archers, however, routed the little Haldians. The Assyrian footmen stabbed them or hacked off their legs as they lay on the ground. Fighting in couples as they always did, the Assyrians entered the gates and fired the unfortunate city, while Ar-a-me', the King of the Haldians, hurrying through the mountains, found himself too late. His forces, in confusion, were driven back into the hills.

Over mountains so high that attendants must needs lead the chariots, the Assyrians then returned to the Cave-of-the-

Shalmaneser at the source of the Tigris. A bull and a ram are led forward for sacrifice before the image of Shalmaneser. A sculptor standing on a block in midstream completes the carving of the image on the rock at the entrance to the grotto. The underground course of the river is shown by means of rectangular openings through which trees protrude and men are seen wading waist-deep and carrying torches. At the right a sentry stands on the hill.

Shalmaneser at the source of the Tigris. Figures from lower picture page 302. Background from a photograph.

River, the source of the sacred Tigris. There the King had his effigy carved on the rock and held a triumphal procession, while soldiers waded knee deep in the dark and icy waters, holding torches aloft to lighten the gloom of the cave.

In spite of this show of power, however, Shalmaneser had not in reality made much impression on Haldia. A new king, Sar-du'rish, replaced A-ra-me' in Armenia, and straightway styled himself King of the World, thus directly flinging a challenge into the teeth of Shalmaneser.

Henceforth, Shalmaneser sent his stout Tartan, Dai'an Ashur, to batter his head in vain against these stubborn warriors while he turned to easier foes, destroying crops and orchards on the pleasant green plains of Babylon, and finally forcing Babylon to pay allegiance to him, thus beginning that union of Babylon and Assyria which was to continue with few interruptions, for all the rest of their history.

The Assyrians attack Por'ga, a city belonging to the Hittite state of Hamath and they use a particularly interesting battering ram shaped like a sow with staring eyes, projecting snout and heavy necklace. All the pictures on page 64 are from the bronze gates of Shalmaneser. For the cities mentioned below see the map page 70.

Having settled matters with Babylon and left Haldia to his Tartan, Shalmaneser now thought the time ripe for stretching out greedy fingers and snatching the spoils of Syria. Crossing the Euphrates, he began the systematic attempt to conquer the nearest towns.

North Syria was now half Hittite and half Aramaean. Gurgum and Hamath were Hittite states; Samal and Damascus were Aramaean. From the oasis of Damascus, for centuries a caravan mart of very great importance, Ben' Ha'dad had made an empire.

In 854 B.C., Shalmaneser advanced, looting frontier cities in Hamath, burning the royal palaces, and marching through orchards of dusky figs along the river Orontes.

Hittite men and women captives and Shalmaneser seated in state. These Hittites wear a short pointed beard instead of the long square beard of the Assyrians. They have pointed shoes instead of the Assyrian sandal; their straight robe is simply fringed in contrast to the heavily fringed Assyrian jacket with diagonal opening at the front.

Real Arabs from the desert such as those who furnished a camel-contingent at the battle of Kar'kar, Aramaeans, Hebrews and all other Semitic tribes came originally from the desert, settled in cities and developed an individual civilization; but the real Arab remained a wanderer and a dweller in tents. (From an Assyrian relief.)

He met no open resistance till he came to the fortress of Kar'kar, but there he was faced at last by a powerful confederacy of tribes headed by Had'ad-e'zer, now the King of Damascus, by Ir-hu-le'ni of Hamath, and Ahab the King of Israel. With them were thousands of chariots, tens-of-thousands of footmen, and even a camel contingent contributed by true Arabs, the wanderers of the desert.

This confederacy gave battle to Shalmaneser, and the mighty King of Assyria found himself soundly whipped, so that, though he boasted a victory on all his future monuments, he had to retreat back home and dared not for many years come westward again into Syria.

Not until twelve years had passed, did he actually come again to raid the lands west of Euphrates.

Of the constantly quarreling kings who kept Syria all

Captives and spoils from Karkar as Shalmaneser boasted of them on his famous bronze gates, a boast ridiculously contradicted by the fact that he dared not for twelve years go again against Syria. The women of this Hittite-Syrian city, like those in the picture opposite, have long hair and are bare-legged with skirts cut up high in front.

From Tyre on its rocky island off the Syrian coast, the tribute of rich Phoenician cities destined for Shalmaneser, is carried to the mainland in boats with prows and sterns shaped like camel's heads. For Jehu's tribute see page 204.

split up, Haz'a-el of Damascus had now become the most powerful. Shalmaneser dared not attack him. He had to content himself with raiding the country around and marching down into Israel with a blustering show of power.

There Je'hu, an army captain, had wiped out all A'hab's line and made himself King in their stead, and he thought to strengthen his claim to the throne by allying himself with Assyria, so he hastened to kiss the ground before the King of Kings while a group of his subjects brought tribute.

Thereafter Shalmaneser went home having accomplished nothing. In spite of his boasts, the world now knew that Assyria would not rule Syria in the days of Shalmaneser.

Phoenician merchant princes adore Shalmaneser. These princes wear turbans bound by long ribbons. They have clinging, double robes and shoes with upturned toes. Their beards are pointed, not square like the Assyrians.

Semiramis, the First Great Queen of Assyria

Shalmaneser's son, Sham'shi-A'dad, ruled only a short time in Asshur, leaving the throne to his infant son, while his wife, the great Queen Sam'-mu-ra'mat, called Se-mir'a-mis by the Greeks, acted as Queen Regent during the youth of the King.

Semiramis was the only great woman who ever ruled in Assyria and she ruled with force and vigor, ever extending her borders toward the Me'di-an hordes in the hills.

So unusual was it for a woman to rule in Asshur, that legends of this great Queen endure to this very day.

After Semiramis, weak successors sat on the throne in Nineveh, often bowing the neck to Babylon. Assyria was in eclipse and, off to the westward in Syria, the smaller nations were left to themselves to grow in riches and power.

In Israel, Jer'o-bo'am II ruled prosperously and long and his people held their heads high, fearing neither Egypt nor Assyria. No man save the prophet A'mos, in those days, saw that Assyria was only for a short time sunk in temporary weakness and would soon come again in her frightfulness to the lands across the Euphrates.

Semiramis, according to legend, was the daughter of a goddess, brought up by doves. She won the heart of the King by her courage; he took her to be his wife, and she became the great warrior Queen of Assyria and Babylon.

Tiglath Pileser III

(746 B.C. TO 726 B.C.)

The vision of Amos was all too true. In 746 B.C., a certain strong official, Tiglath Pileser III, usurped the throne in Asshur and having reconquered Babylon, he marched off westward to Syria, not daring to attack Assyria's bold foe, Haldia, behind her mountain ramparts in far away Armenia, but thinking to break forever the influence gained by Haldia over the Syrian kings.

A powerful coalition advanced to meet Tiglath Pileser in the hills near the upper Euphrates, but they were disgracefully routed, and the King of Haldia only escaped by a lonely flight on a mare.

Having thus left on the Armenians his never-to-be-forgotten fear, Tiglath Pileser at last crossed the river Euphrates, spreading terror everywhere. If Assyria had failed in the hills, Haldia had failed in the plains, and certain Syrian kings hastened to come and embrace the feet of that glowing flame, Tiglath Pileser. Bar Re'kub of Samal said proudly, "I ran at the wheel of my lord, the King of Assyria, even in the midst of most mighty kings, lords of silver and lords of gold."

Almost all of northern Syria now bowed to Tiglath Pileser and acknowledged the power of his might. And whenever he conquered a people, he carried the natives away and brought in foreign tribes. Mountaineers he made to settle in the plains. Bankers and artisans he made to work in the fields.

Tiglath Pileser III makes war. (From his palace at Nimrud.) For his campaign against Rezin see page 221.

An Aramaean queen of the time of Bar Rekub and the great Bar Rekub himself. These pictures show both the facial features and the high state of art of this intelligent Semitic tribe. Reliefs from Samal now in the Berlin Museum.

Rude wanderers from the desert he placed in the cultured cities; and from this confusion of tribes grew that mixed race of people who were the later Syrians.

In Israel all was confusion. Still recalling the ancient days of Egypt's imperial power, Israel first looked to Egypt for aid and then sent gifts to Assyria.

"Israel is like a silly dove, devoid of understanding!" thundered the prophet, Hosea; "they call unto Egypt and then go to Assyria. They make a covenant with Assyria and then send gifts to Egypt."

Nevertheless, as soon as Tiglath Pileser went home and withdrew the terror of his majesty from the nations west of Euphrates, they straightway forgot their fear and began their quarrels anew. Pe'kah, King of Israel, joined with Re'-zin, King of Damascus, and went against A'haz of Judah, and Ahaz was so frightened that he sent in a panic to Tiglath Pileser, begging aid against his two foes. In vain did the

SEA OF THE SETTING SUN (MEDITERRANEAN SEA)

Other Hittite Cities and Settlements of various Barbarian Greek Tribes

Gurgum (Hittite)

Samal (Hittite) • Carchemish (Hittite)

Euphrates River

Aleppo

To ASHUR and ASSYRIA

Orontes

Karkar (Aramean)

Hamath (Hittite)

Island City of Arvad (Phoenician)

Samara

Kadesh (Hittite)

Byblus (Phoenician)

SYRIA

Sidon (Phoenician) • Damascus (Aramean)

Tyre (Phoenician)

Acche

Mt.Carmel

Dor

Samaria

Ashdod

Jerusalem

Gath

Gaza

Jezreel (Hebrew)

JUDAH ISRAEL

Jordan Dead Sea

AMMON

MOAB

EDOM

←To the Delta Country of Egypt

See the map of the Growth of the Assyrian Empire on page 14.

prophet I-sa'iah cry out against such a step, calling Rezin and Pekah two dying stumps of fire brands whose flame would soon burn out! Ahaz stripped gold and silver from his palace and the temple and sent it to Tiglath Pileser, saying, "I am thy servant and thy son, come and save me!"

And Tiglath Pileser came. He killed the unruly Rezin, impaled his advisors on stakes, hacked down his gardens and orchards, and made all central Syria a dependency of Asshur. Pekah of Israel he deposed and he made a certain Hoshea king in Pekah's stead.

Then Ahaz of Judah, hastened to come to Damascus and kiss the Great King's feet.

Under Tiglath Pileser III, Assyria had become again a mighty nation of warriors, slaying, burning, impaling, putting out eyes, and cutting off ears, and domineering completely over the smaller states that lay west of the Euphrates.

Ten years later in 722 B.C., Ho-she'a, King of Israel, rebelled against Assyria; and Shalmaneser V came and took Samaria, crushing the land forever, carrying off the ten tribes of Israel and replacing them with the foreign tribes who were the unfriendly Samaritans with whom the Jews had no dealings in the later days of Jesus.

Shalmaneser, however, had little joy of his conquest; for while he still fought in Israel, one of his generals arose, usurped the throne in Assyria, and was hailed by his warriors as King. This general was Sar'gon II, King of the Universe, King of the four quarters of the world!

Sargon II approaches the superb entrance of his new city, Dur Shar-ruk'en, or Sargonsburg. The gates are guarded by human-headed winged bulls and decorated with gay colored tiles. The use of the arch is typically Assyrian.

The Splendors of Sargon II and Sennacherib

(722 B.C. TO 681 B.C.)

The Assyrian armies were now world-feared. Sargon, "the mighty hero, clothed with terror, who smashed all lands like earthen vessels," was soon free to devote himself to the gentler arts of peace. Near Nineveh he erected a city, Dur Sharruken, the splendid, with a hundred and fifty towers, eight gateways, and a magnificent royal palace, towering high above the walls.

Through the great central gateway, guarded by huge winged bulls and decorated above with brightly enameled bricks, Sargon often rode in joy of heart and with beaming countenance, while the city swarmed with merrymakers who bought sweet-meats and snow-cooled drinks and admired the wondrous beauties of the City of the King.

On such a crowd of merrymakers the news was one

day borne that Sargon, the Great, was dead; Sargon, the Great, was murdered! Sen-nach'er-ib, his son, was now the king in his stead.

In Palestine all was rejoicing. Sargon had been their oppressor. But Isaiah cried in Jerusalem:—"Rejoice not, O all Palestina, because the rod of him that smote thee is broken; for out of the serpent's root shall come forth a basilisk and his fruit shall be a fiery dragon!"

A fiery dragon indeed was Sennacherib, the new King. In eight long, savage campaigns, he struck his foes with lightning. Like a whirlwind, he came to the sea-coast.

Strong walled cities bowed before him. In terror, they called upon Egypt, and the King of Egypt sent to their aid bowmen, chariots, and horses, but Sennacherib scattered Egypt; he took their princes captive.

As for Hez'e-ki'ah, the Jew, who did not submit to his yoke, forty-six of his strong-walled cities, by bringing up siege engines and leveling with battering rams, Sennacherib took. Twenty thousand people, great and small, male and female, horses, mules, asses, camels, cattle, and sheep without number, he brought away and counted as spoil. Hezekiah himself, like a caged bird, he shut up in Jerusalem.

Fifty talents of gold, eight hundred talents of silver, jewels, couches of ivory, elephant hide, his daughters, his harem, his male and female musicians, Hezekiah sent to Sennacherib. To accept servitude he despatched his messengers.

Then Sennacherib turned against Babylon, to punish Mer-o'dach Bal'a-dan, rebellious Prince of the Swamps.

And, Merodach-Baladan, fearing the roar of his mighty arms and the onset of his terrible battle, gathered together the gods of his whole land, loaded them into his ships, and fled like a bird to an island, which is in the midst of the sea.

"Son of a murderer, prop of a wicked devil!" Sennacherib, in his rage, called the rebellious Chal-de'an. His brothers he seized; he brought them forth as spoil from the marshes, the canebrakes, and swamps. His cities he burned with fire. On his ally, the King of Elam, he poured out terror and ruin.

He went against those of Elam whose abodes were set like the eagles on the heights of the mountain peaks. Like a strong ox he advanced; he went before his warriors. Gullies, mountain torrents, waterfalls, dangerous cliffs he surmounted, being borne in his carrying-chair. Where the way was too steep for his chair, he climbed along on foot. His chariot was pulled up by ropes.

Like a young gazelle, he mounted the highest peak. Wherever he found a resting place he sat down on a mountain boulder and drank cold water from the water skin.

The people of Elam he carried off; the people of Babylon he conquered together with their gods.

But when Me-ro'dach Bal'a-dan died, Shu'zu-bu, another Chaldean, from the swamp-lands by the sea-coast, made himself King of Babylon. Into the marshes he descended and made rebellion there. He gathered to him run-aways, murderers, and robbers. They rested like rats in the fen-lands.

"A weakling hero who has no knees, a slave!" Sennacherib roared. He surrounded Shuzubu's host. He pressed him to the life. Through fear and hunger, Shuzubu fled to Elam.

The King of Elam gathered his army and camp, collected his chariots and wagons, and hitched his horses and mules. An enormous vassal host he called to his side; great masses of

Sennacherib leads his army in his royal chariot beneath his state umbrella.

warriors gathered and took the road to Babylon. Like
swarms of locusts in springtime, they kept coming steadily
onward against the King of Assyria. With the dust of
their feet covering the face of the heavens like the appearing of a storm-cloud, they drew up in battle array before
an Assyrian city on the banks of the river Tigris.

Sennacherib prayed for victory over the mighty foe. Like
a lion he raged. He put on his coat of mail. His helmet,
emblem of victory, he placed upon his head. His great battle-
chariot he mounted in the anger of his heart. His mighty
bow he seized in his hands; his javelin he grasped. Against
all the hosts of his enemies, he raised his voice like a storm.
Like A-dad', the storm-god, he roared. Front and rear, he
pressed them, surrounding the ranks of the foe!

The nobles of the King of Elam who wear the golden
girdle-dagger, and whose wrists are encircled with bracelets,
like fat steers with hobbled feet, he cut down and speedily
slew. His prancing steeds plunged into streams of blood as

Workmen carry ropes, tools, and levers for the building of Sennacherib's palace. Behind is a hilly country with
vines, pine and pomegranate trees. Below the mountain is a river and at the right a village with dwellings whose
roofs are rounded or shaped like sugar-loaves. This is the only representation which has ever been discovered,
showing what the homes of the common people looked like in ancient days in Assyria.

Reconstruction of the grand entrance to Sennacherib's wonderful palace at Kou-yun'jik by Fergusson based upon excavations of the site. The airy columns and soaring terraces show quite an advance in building over Sargon's heavier palace. Every inch of space on the lower part of the building was profusely decorated with bas-reliefs.

into the waters of a river. With the bodies of their warriors, he filled the plain like grass!

The King of Elam, together with the King of Babylon and princes of Chaldea, abandoned their tents and fled; they fled like young pigeons pursued!

From the Upper Sea of the Setting Sun to the Lower Sea of the Rising Sun, Sennacherib's weapons were powerful.

Sennacherib silenced his foes; and rich in the power of his victories, he turned to enlarging Nineveh, where from of old, his fathers had exercised lordship over Assyria. He laid out streets; he widened the squares; he dug a canal; he set out trees, he made bright the streets and avenues and caused them to shine like the day. Captive Chaldeans and Ara-

Round boats of the type still in use on the Tigris and Euphrates, carry building material for Sennacherib's palace. Oarsmen steer adroitly between the fishes, the crab, and the men afloat on inflated animals' skins, who are fishing, patiently waiting for a bite and carrying the fishes already caught in baskets on their backs. See page 19.

maeans whom his hands had conquered in war, he forced to carry the building basket and mould the bricks of clay. He raised a platform of stone, and thereon he built a palace of ivory, ebony and cedar, the "Palace-without-a-rival."

Lions of shining bronze exceeding glorious, mighty bull-colossi of bronze and colored enamel, cow-colossi of alabaster, clothed with exuberant strength, whose bodies shone like bright day, he set up as posts at the doors.

For the housing of battle-steeds, mules, colts, riding-camels, chariots, wagons, carts, quivers, bows and arrows, he built an armory, and he enlarged the Court of the Gate for the exercising of horses. Thither he caused to be brought the tribute of the lands, the wealth of the distant Medes, whose tribute none among the Kings, his fathers, had ever received, together with the wagons and riding chariots of the King of Elam, and the King of Babylon and Chal-de'a.

For twenty-three years Sennacherib reigned in Nineveh, but in the twenty-third year of his reign, rebellion arose against him. To gain the kingship, two royal sons plotted evil. As Sennacherib worshipped in the temple, they slew him with the sword and fled away to Armenia; and E'sar-had'don came and reigned in his father's stead.

Greater Power and Sudden Collapse
(680 B.C. TO 612 B.C.)

"I was fierce as a lion!" cried Esarhaddon; "and my liver was enraged! Like a flying sis'in-nu bird for the overthrow of mine enemies, I opened out my forces!"

And he set out to conquer Egypt, once the Queen of the World, she whom Assyrian kings had long desired to subdue to prove themselves lords of the earth. He pushed his way into the Delta, defeated Ta-har'ka, the negro king, and forced twenty-eight Delta princes to bow the knee before him.

"King of the Kings of Egypt," Esarhaddon called himself and his fame went down in history as that of the first Assyrian King to humble the once mighty Egypt.

As'sur-ba'ni-pal, Esarhaddon's son, was not like his father, a fighter. Torchlight processions, like rainbows, among the trees of his gardens, the pleasures of life at court, the collection of a great library of 22,000 clay tablets, and the lordly sport of hunting appealed to the King more than battles. In the reign of Assurbanipal, Assyria reached its height in luxury, culture, and art.

A great day was that when the King declared a royal hunt. Fierce lions, dreadful children of the mountains, were carried in wooden cages to an open space in the plain. Soldiers stood by, shield to shield, to prevent the escape of the beasts.

This and the three following illustrations are copies of reliefs from Assurbanipal's palace at Nineveh.

As'sur-ban'i-pal seized his bow and stepped into his chariot while the signal was given with a breathless thrill to open the doors of the cages and let the lions loose.

In a moment the King was surrounded; lions surrounded his chariot. He seized a fierce beast by the ears! He pierced him with his girdle dagger! He shot arrows from his terrible bow! He crushed the skull of a lion with the club that was in his hand! He shattered the might of those lions!

Over the bodies of five great beasts he brought an offering to Ishtar; he poured out wine unto Asshur, King of all the

gods, and to Ishtar, lady of battles, who decreed him a life of heroes.

A banquet followed in the palace. In a sheltered, vine-covered arbor, surrounded by graceful date palms, the king reclined on a couch, with a gorgeously embroidered shawl thrown over his outstretched limbs. Before him sat his queen, upright in her throne-like chair; nearby stood attendants with fly-whisks, while servants from the royal kitchen constantly passed to and fro, bringing savory and tempting dishes, and maidens from the palace scattered blossoms about or crowned the king with flowers.

So dwelt Assurbanipal before whose valiant bow kings

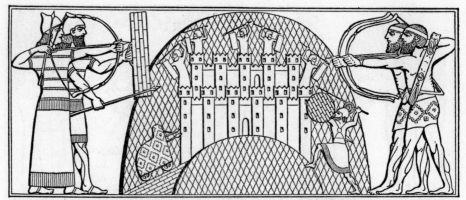

Siege of a Median City. The steep slope where the battering ram stands and the rounded mounds show very mountainous country. The Elamites, Kassites and Persians lived with the Medes in these mountains south-east of Assyria.

and lions were powerless; but Assurbanipal's sons were no such mighty hunters. They seized neither kings nor lions by their ears or by their tails! Under them, Egypt broke away and became independent again. Hordes of Medes from the mountains came down and harried the land, and Chaldeans from the Sea-lands, that ever-turbulent province, came up out of their marshes, and took city after city.

Nab-o-po-las'sar, Viceroy of Chal-de'a, made himself King of Babylon and marched up the river Euphrates to join

Fighting in the Babylonian marshes, the sea-lands of the Chaldeans. The Chaldeans, some with women crouching in their boats are at the left; the Assyrians are at the right. Above, a raft filled with Chaldean prisoners is poled by an Assyrian soldier. Among reeds taller than their heads, Assyrian cavalrymen advance. Here in these marshes along the coast, a restless rebellious people had long given the Assyrians and the Babylonians much trouble. Mer-o'dach Bal'a-dan, a Chaldean Prince was a constant rebel against Sargon and Sennacherib. (See pages 72, 228.) From this race came the new Chaldean Empire and the conquerors Nabopolassar and Neb'u-chad-nez'zar.

The wedding of Amytis and Nebuchadnezzar unites the Medes of the mountains and the Chaldeans of the marshlands against Assyria. For the fall of Nineveh see page 482. For Nebuchadnezzar, see pages 322 and 323.

Cy-ax'e-res, King of the Medes. Before the city of Asshur the two kings met. Good will and alliance was established between them. Neb-u-chad-nez'zar, the first born, chief son of Nabopolassar, Prince of the low-lying Marshlands, who had borne bricks on his head and carried mortar with the workmen for the building up of Babylon, was married to Am'y-tis, Princess of the Medes, a royal maid from the hills.

Together the Medes and Chaldeans went and laid siege to Nineveh. In spite of her mighty walls, her ditches flowing with water, Nineveh, the all-powerful, who had built up her empire by bloodshed, fell before the foe. She was turned into mounds and ploughlands and left but an heap in the desert. From distant ends of the earth, men cried:

"Woe to the bloody city that is all full of lies and robbery; that has multiplied her merchants above the stars of heaven! She is empty and void and waste! Her people is scattered; her captains have fled; her nobles dwell in the dust!"

A Median chief presenting a model of a city (from Botta and Flandin).

Figures in glazed tile with which Neb'-u-chad-nez'zar beautified Babylon; a lion from his Procession Street, and a dragon with body and head of a snake, forelegs of a lion and hindlegs of an eagle. This dragon was the symbol of Mar'duk, the chief god adored by Nebuchadnezzar and it adorned the Ishtar Gate of Marduk's temple in Babylon.

III

The Chaldean Empire in Babylon

Nebuchadnezzar, the Chaldean of the Sea-Lands.

(605-562 B.C.)

Cameo portrait of Nebuchadnezzar.

Once again Babylon lifted her head as Queen in the Land of Two Rivers. Nineveh had fallen. Loud rose rejoicings in Judah, in Syria, and the West.

But tyrants were to issue from Babylon even as they had from Nineveh. Nab-o-po-las'sar soon sent his son, the young crown-prince Nebuchadnezzar, to conquer the nations of Syria.

Steep trails and unopened paths the Warrior-Prince traversed; journeys he made without water till he came to the Upper Sea. The unruly he overthrew. He bound as captives his enemies; Je-hoi'a-kim of Judah he forced to pay yearly tribute; and at Car'che-mish by the Euphrates he smote Pharaoh Ne'cho of Egypt who has risen up like a flood overwhelming Judah and Syria.

"Pharaoh King of Egypt is but a noise," men cried; "he has passed the time appointed!"

And Nebuchadnezzar ceased not from following after Pharaoh till news arrived in his camp that Nabopolassar

82

Nebuchadnezzar looks with kingly pride on the Hanging Gardens which he has built for his Median queen.

was dead and he must return to be crowned King in Babylon.

Once more he greeted Am'y-tis, his fair young Median Queen. That she might not pine for her homeland-hills in the midst of Babylon's plain, he builded gardens mountain-high, terrace piled on terrace, with flash of fountains, shade of trees, and fragrance of pomegranates.

In three years' time, however, King Ze-de-ki'ah of Judah, and other small allied kings, stirred up by the new Pharaoh, Hoph'ra, rebelled again against Babylon. Then came Ne-buchadnezzar and took Jerusalem. From the Lower Sea to the Upper Sea, all Kings now owed him allegiance.

To receive the homage of the conquered, the products of mountains and seas, he looked to the welfare of Babylon. He built and restored her temples. The shrine of mighty

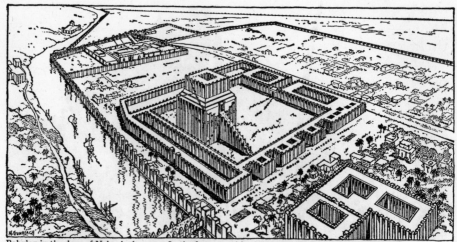

Babylon in the days of Nebuchadnezzar. In the foreground is the great temple of Marduk (the Tower of Babel) with other buildings in the sacred enclosure. Beyond at the bend in the river, are the Palace of Nebuchadnezzar and the Hanging Gardens. Connecting palace and temple at the right of the sacred enclosure, is the famous Procession Street. Much of Babylon has been excavated and visitors may see remains of Nebuchadnezzar's work.

Marduk whom he worshipped above all gods, he made to shine like the sun; he adorned it with glistening gold.

The great walls of Babylon, Im-gur Bel and Ni-mit'ti Bel, he completed. He stationed at the threshold of their gates strong wild bulls of bronze and terrible serpents standing upright. That the shaft of battle might not reach Imgur Bel, he built an outer wall mountain high and dug its moat toward the east. For the great lord Marduk he built a Procession Street. From the Shining Gate to the Boulevard, he paved it with brick and stone. He raised it up on a terrace. He made its roadway broad. Between Imgur Bel and the Outer wall he built himself a dwelling for the astonished gaze of the peoples. From his palace, the Brilliant Abode, Nebuchadnezzar issued his royal edicts and lordly decrees, worshipping mighty Marduk, lord of all the gods.

Babylon Is Fallen!
(539 B.C.)

The sons and successors of Nebuchadnezzar ruled very weakly in Babylon; in time men sought Na-bon'i-dus, who was no Chaldean of the Sea-lands, but of old Babylonian blood, of the proud ancient race of Su'mer. Men threw themselves at his feet. They made him rule the land.

And Na-bon'i-dus ruled well. Under him great Babylon prospered. Her crowded bazaars were rich in merchandise of gold, in carpets and woolens and linens; in cinnamon and spices; in horses and chariots and slaves. Her rich men walked the streets in long woolen robes and turbans, each carrying a walking stick with a handle carved like a flower.

Nevertheless, the new king's heart went after Sin and Sha'-mash and the ancient gods of Sumer, and he served Marduk of Babylon only with empty show. Therefore the priests of Marduk did not love Nabonidus. Moreover, the Persians, a strong, simple folk who had tended their flocks for centuries in the steep heights to the eastward, suddenly found their quarrelsome tribes united beneath the leadership of Cy'rus, their strong young king. They conquered the Medes, and came down from their hills bent on the conquest of Babylon.

Nearer and nearer drew Cyrus, his troops like the waters of a river; but Nabonidus stayed in Tema, an old man, pious and kindly, dwelling in quiet peace. He left his son, Bel-shaz'zar in charge of affairs in Babylon and came not up to the city even in Festival Month.

Stronghold after stronghold opened its doors to Cyrus. Belshazzar, advancing to meet him, was sent back home in flight. And then, in the seventeenth year of his reign Naboni-dus came to Babylon. He came in the Festival Month and brought many strange gods with him. And the priests and lovers of Marduk rose up in anger and rage. They opened the gates to Cyrus. Without a skirmish or battle, Cyrus entered Babylon. He took Nabonidus prisoner; Belshazzar, his son, he slew.

With joy and rejoicing, Cyrus took up his residence in the royal palace in Babylon. In all Sumer and Ak'kad he per-

Persian archers of the army that conquered Babylon, wearing the beautifully draped Persian robe, which the Persians took from the Medes and which differed from Babylonian garments in the grace of its softly draped folds. A frieze of bright colored bricks from the Palace of Da-ri'us, Su'sa. See Vol. III, page 166.

mitted no unfriendly treatment; he inflicted no dishonorable servitude. The Jews and all captive peoples he permitted to return to their homes to worship their gods as they chose; for such was the custom of the Persians.

All kings dwelling in royal halls from the Upper to the Lower Sea, all kings of the West-country who dwelt in tents, now brought their taxes to Cyrus, lover of A'hu-ra Maz'da, the great god of light and Truth.

"Babylon is fallen!" men cried; "Babylon is fallen, is fallen; the great city, the mighty city, she that sat as a Queen, that dwelt upon many waters! Babylon is fallen!

"A sword is upon the Chaldeans and on the people of Babylon, her princes and her wise-men! A sword is upon her horses, her chariots, and mingled people! Her broad walls are utterly broken! Her high gates are burned with fire! At the noise of the taking of Babylon, all the earth is moved!"

Fallen forever now were Babylon and Assyria, heirs to Sumer and Akkad. They who had taught the world how to make organized warfare, with all the gruesome horrors attendant on wars of greed, they who had given the world its first code of laws, and its first business methods, were never to rule again. Henceforth it was a Persian who bore the lordly titles, "King of the World, the Great King, King of the four quarters of the earth, King of the Universe."

Abraham and Sarah in the streets of Ur. Abraham, the black-bearded Semite, whose race came out of the desert and conquered the native Sumerians, is in sharp contrast to the Sumerian men of Ur who had their faces and heads shaved. The costumes of Abraham and Sarah are taken from the Egyptian wall-painting on page 98 and the Sumerians from statuettes reproduced on page 88. The dagger worn by the Sumerian was discovered in a grave at Ur. Its sheath is of gold, its handle of lapis lazuli, studded with gold. The little gold vanity case of the lady, containing tweezers, stiletto, and spoon, was likewise discovered in a grave at Ur. See page 15.

IV

Hebrew Wanderers*

Abraham, Chief of the Tribe

(ABOUT 2100 B. C.)

In the crowded city of Ur, where the smooth-faced native Su-me′ri-an, close-shaven and bald of head, rubbed shoulders day by day, with the dark-haired, bearded Sem′ite, dignified son of the desert, dwelt a certain Semite, named Abraham, with Te′rah, his father, and Sarah, his wife. Mid the narrow, winding streets, Abraham passed the lady of fashion

*Where truth ends and legend begins in the early stories of the Bible, whether Abraham, the patriarchs and Moses were heroes of great epic tales belonging to literature rather than history, cannot now be stated with certainty. The story here given follows the Bible, which in its general outlines at least, presents facts, and is as reliable as any other traditional history told by word of mouth and not written down for years after its occurrence. The Bible is a whole collection of literature—history, poetry, drama, fiction,—representing the best of the thoughts of the Hebrew race which gave the world its first conception of one God. The various books of the Bible were written in widely different periods, worked over and edited again and again, and woven into one great mosaic, from which it is difficult today to extract the separate documents and give them accurate dates.

A Semitic prince of the race of Abraham and his Sumerian secretary (2700 B.C.).   The Prince, the central figure wearing a cap, is a Semite as his beard shows.   Three of his attendants are also Semites, having long hair and beards, but his secretary is a Sumerian, beardless and shaven of head.   (From the Prince's seal, British Museum.)

in her long fringed robe, daintily fingering the little gold vanity case that dangled from her belt. He passed the gentleman of fashion with his ornamental sword of gold and lapis lazuli. He saw beggar and prince, merchant, soldier, craftsman and

Statuettes of a Sumerian man and a Sumerian woman.   Note the large eyes and shaven head of the man.   The woman is of about the period of Abraham.   She wears a gold necklace and is dressed in the typical Sumerian dress, with embroidered or woven bands.   The original is in the Louvre, Paris.

priest; for Ur of the Chal'dees in ancient Mes'o-po-ta'mia, was a very important center in the busy lanes of trade. Here boats from the Eu-phra'tes met caravans from the desert; there was noise of camels and donkeys, with bustle of drivers and merchants, busy bazaars reëchoing with the noisy garble of mixed Semitic and Sumerian tongues, great wealth, great pride, great prosperity, even regular postmen, arriving post haste with cylindrical letters of clay, done up in clay envelopes, addressed in wedge-shaped figures.

For fifteen hundred years, Ur had ruled the surrounding country like other city states. Before the proud days of Bab'y-lon and Nin'e-veh, she had even once ruled an empire; but the desert-folk had been drifting in, Abraham's kinsmen and forefathers, they who had wandered for ages over the sands of Arabia, seeking the scanty grass to feed their herds and sheep.

Gradually the Semites won more and more space in Chal-de'a, finally gaining control of Ur two hundred years before Abraham's day. Ur, under rule of the Semites, however, was still an important city, whither men came crowding to worship the moon-god, Nan'nar-Sin, and Nin'gal, the moon-goddess. In the center of the city above the clay-brick

Ur-Engur, King of Ur, 2300 B.C., instructed by the moon-god, Nannar, to build the ziggurat at Ur. A beautiful carving in relief on limestone. Ur-Engur pours libations into a vase of dates and palm leaves, before the moon-god Nannar, on the right, and the moon-goddess, Nin-gal, on the left. The moon-god offers Ur-Engur an architect's coiled line and measuring rod. These were the gods of Ur which Abraham refused to worship.

The great Zig'gu-rat or temple tower of Ur as it is today, a solid mountain of mud brick, built by Ur-Engur, King of Ur, about 2300 B.C., two hundred years before Abraham's day, and rebuilt by Nab-o-ni'dus, last King of Babylon about 550 B.C.   Every city of Babylonia possessed a similar staged tower with a shrine to its particular god on top. The stairways can still be seen in the same position as those shown on page 91.   The shrine to the moon-god crowned this tower and the ruins in front are the house of the moon-goddess.

dwellings, rose the huge temple tower of Nannar, a massive pile of receding steps, beneath which clustered Ningal's house and a jumbled mass of buildings, all enclosed within the temple walls.

But as Abraham saw the worshippers daily making their way to the temple of the moon-god and the house of the moon-goddess, serving, with elaborate ceremonies, the gods of earth and sky created by their own fancies, and blindly looking to them as the power that governed life, there stirred in his soul a rebellion against all those wild superstitions. He began to grope after God, if haply he might find him,— one living God alone, a real, vital presence who should speak living words to his heart. And he and his wife, Sarah, and his father, Terah, and Lot, his brother's son, would not

The Ziggurat or House of the Mountain, as Abraham saw it in his day. Elaborate processions of priests and worshippers climbed the stairs and marched around the succeeding stages to the shrine of the moon-god on top. The Sumerians came into the flat plains of Mesopotamia from a mountain country where they built their temples on mountain tops. So they reared the ziggurats, artificial hills, that their gods might have their thrones as of old, on the mountain tops. This picture is taken from the same view as the ruins on page 90.

follow the gods of their fathers; for they left the way of their ancestors and worshiped the God whom they knew. But to worship a real, living God, within the shadow of the temple tower devoted to dead stone idols, and constantly confused in mind by the sight of priestly processions passing in gorgeous splendor up the temple steps, was far too great a task. So the Lord said unto Abraham: "Get thee out of thy country unto a land which I will show thee."

And Abraham obeyed; he went forth out of Ur, with Sarah, Lot and Terah, not knowing whither he went, but seeking the Promised Land, turning his back on Ur with all its material glories and seeking a city which had foundations, whose builder and maker was God. The four journeyed northward and westward, dwelling in tents, as their

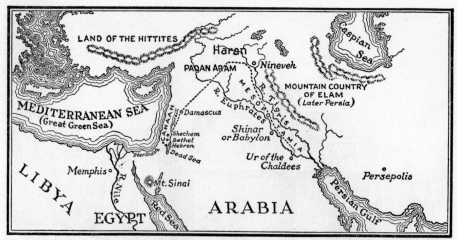

The dotted line shows how Abraham, Lot and Sarah, wandered from Ur up to Haran in Padan Aram, then down through Canaan to Shechem. For a true story of how the chiefs of Canaan lived in the days of Abraham and his son and grandson see the story of Sinuhe's flight from Egypt and his years spent in the household of just such a sheikh as Abraham, Vol. I, pp. 140-151. See also Vol. I, pp. 138, 139.

fathers had done in the desert land of Arabia, tarrying until Terah died in the green plains of Pa′dan-A′ram, then leaving Mesopotamia and wandering into Ca′naan,—a land of rocks, ravines, and barren, gray, stony moorland, cleft by the river Jordan with its rugged mountain range.

And Abraham passed through the land, journeying ever southward, till there burst all at once upon his view the beautiful vale of She′chem, fertile as a garden, gay with

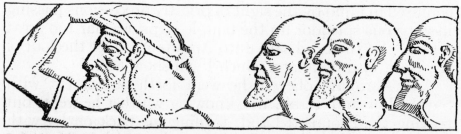

Typical Amorites of the sort found by Abraham in Canaan.   The original inhabitants of Canaan, Canaanites and Amorites, were races very closely akin.   They were Semites like the Hebrews, having the upper lip shaven, but wearing a long, rather pointed and projecting beard, in contrast to the clean-shaven faces of Egyptians and the long, heavy, braided and curled, square beard of the Assyrians and Babylonians. The Amorites seem to have been distinguished from Canaanites and Israelites by having the hair on their heads cropped very close, while Canaanites and Israelites wore long hair. A carving from the tomb of Ramses II, at Thebes (1225 B.C.).

Abraham, Sarah and Lot arriving in Shechem, the valley between Mts. Ebal and Ger'i-zim. Landscape copied from a photograph. It was in this valley that Joseph's brethren kept the flocks of Jacob.

gushing streams, and sheltered in quiet peace beneath twin mountain peaks. And Abraham pitched his tent under the oaks of Mo'reh, in the blooming vale of Shechem. And the Lord appeared unto Abraham and said: "Unto thy seed will I give this land." And Abraham's heart was lifted up, and at Shechem he gathered stones and builded an altar unto God.

And the Ca'naan-ite and the Am'o-rite were then in the land, black-bearded Semitic races who, from the dawn of history, had possessed the sea-coast and the hill-country west of the river Jordan. And they dwelt in dirty, walled towns, where they crudely tried to copy the pottery and

The ruins of a Canaanite castle of Abraham's time, recently excavated at Me-gidd'o, an old Bible city (Joshua 12:21, 17:11). The skeletons at Taanach referred to in the paragraph below were found when Taanach was excavated, the mother still wearing her jewelry and trinkets and surrounded by dishes and household utensils.

crafts of Babylon and Egypt. Their houses were built of clay with a camel's head on the roof to protect them and bring them luck; and if one of the frail things fell, they took no trouble to clean up the heap, but built anew on the ruins. When one collapsed at Ta'a-nach, burying five small children in company with their mother who was just preparing a meal, the people left the mound as it was and built a new home on top. Houses were small, towns were small, streets were miry and dirty. Even the castles of kings who ruled the dirty villages were made of simple clay brick with hard trodden earth for the floors and flat roofs of rushes and mud, that rested on wooden

A scarab or stone image of a beetle made in Abraham's time, about 2000 B. C., and found at Gez'er in Palestine. Chairs must have looked like this and women must have dressed like this in Abraham's day in Canaan.

pillars. Nine rooms surrounding an open court with a cistern in the center was, in Abraham's day, a palace fit for a king.

And the favorite gods of these people were the spirits who dwelt in the trees and the fields, who made the grain to

A mud-brick house such as Abraham saw in Canaan with no windows and a flat roof of rushes and hard-beaten earth laid on wooden cross-beams. Light is let in through the roof by means of a clay tube tapering from both ends to the center. On the roof is a camel's skull to bring good luck. Charms and magic amulets were very common in Canaan.

The pottery jars with plain designs of lines, are copied from jars of this period dug up at Gezer, an old Canaanite city, mentioned in the Bible (Joshua 10:33). The child's toy ram with front legs and hind legs in one piece, is likewise copied exactly from one dug up at Gezer (see page 336 for other toy animals from Gezer).

The men have been playing a game like checkers. The limestone checkerboard which one holds up was used in Gezer in Abraham's day and recently found there along with the draughtsmen which lie on the ground before the men. The chair with lion-shaped feet is copied from the one shown on page 334.

The man who sits in the chair is an Amorite as his close-cropped hair and long beard show. (See the lower picture on page 332.) The man in the doorway with long hair and beard is a Canaanite as are also the woman and child. The man with the tall cap and pigtail and shoes with upturned toes is a Hittite (see page 337). These three races were the ones Abraham found in Canaan when he arrived. The Canaanites and Amorites were very much alike and very much like the Hebrews.

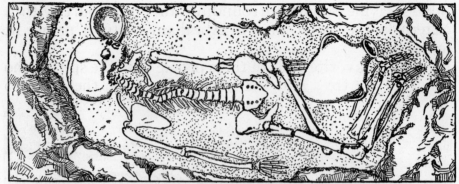

A Canaanite foundation sacrifice from a house in Gezer.   The Canaanites thought it necessary to sacrifice a human life in order to guard a newly built house from evil spirits.   This skeleton is that of an old lady who was buried in the walls of a house in Gezer, along with two vessels of food.   In Megiddo and other Canaanite strongholds skeletons of men, women, and babies have been found built like this right into the walls.

grow and gave fertility to the land. Ba'als, the Canaanites called their gods and they worshipped them with savage rites; with noisy, drunken feasting and often with slaying their first born sons on the altars in their high places beneath tall sacred poles. Moreover, they bought the goodwill of their Baals by burying human beings in the foundations of their houses.   Their superstitions were savage; their

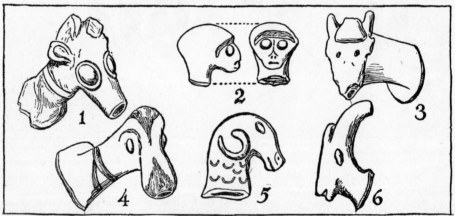

Canaanite models of animals found in Gezer, and probably in many cases children's toys.   One or two were found with a hole drilled through one leg, which might have been for the child to drag them by.   They are as rudely made as if a child had modelled them. Canaanites and Hebrews alike, had little ability in art. The eyes are usually made by sticking on two little balls of clay.   Less often, they are two holes prodded with the end of a stick.   Number 1 is a cow of red pottery with a white collar around its neck. 2 is an ape. 3 is another cow; the triangle on its forehead is its forelock. 4 is a duck. 5 is a ram, the scallops representing wool. 6 is a goat.

arts were rude imitation.

Already these Canaanites were well mixed with Hit'tites from the mountains of Asia. The Hittites were stern high-landers with slant eyes and yellow skins. Beneath their conical caps, their hair hung down in pigtails and they were clad in short belted tunics and boots with upturned toes.

Abraham could see cara-vans go forth from the Canaanite cities. Beside long lines of donkeys walked Canaanite men and women in gay-colored, figured woolen clothing, the men having san-dals on their feet and the women wearing shoes.

Then Abraham removed and went to dwell at Beth'el.

A Hittite warrior with conical cap and pig-tail, from a Hittite sculpture dug up at the old Hittite city of Sin-jer'li. He is clad in the typical short woolen jacket and tall boots, with upturned toes. He carries a very long sword and spear and the figure 8 shield.

The Hittites, or children of Heth, were a con-federacy of a number of different races; but the most striking type was almost like the Chinese, with slant eyes, and pig-tails hanging down their backs. See pages 50, 104-5; also Vol. I, p. 228.

And God was as real to him as the men who passed his tent, a friend to whom he could talk as simply as a child.

And there was a famine in the land and Abraham went into Egypt. And he sojourned there in the fertile lands of the Delta. And when he came back to Bethel, he and Lot had grown rich in flocks and herds and tents; and the fol-lowers of their tribe had greatly increased in Egypt.

And there was strife concerning pasture-lands between the herdsmen of Lot and the herdsmen of Abraham. And Abraham said unto Lot: "Let there be no strife between me and thee, and between my herdsmen and thy herdsmen, for

Canaanites going down into Egypt with their wives and children,—the only known portraits of Canaanites of Abraham's time. Painted on the walls of a nobleman's tomb at Be'ni Has'an in Egypt. Abraham's caravan must have looked like this when he went down into Egypt. The clothing of the men and women was gay-figured heavy wool in contrast to the Egyptians who wore only washable linen. Egyptians thought these Asiatics barbarous people because they wore clothing which could not be washed. The beards of the Israelites distinguish them from the clean-shaven Egyptians. The women and children wear shoes; the men wear sandals.

we be brethren. Separate thyself, I pray thee, from me. If thou wilt take the left hand, then I will go to the right."

And Lot lifted up his eyes and chose the plain of Jordan, that was green as a watered garden. And he dwelled in the cities of the plain and pitched his tent toward Sod'om. But Abraham crossed a vast stretch of gray and stony moorland blazing beneath the sun, and he journeyed south to Hebron, a town in a narrow valley surrounded by rocky hills. There he pitched his tent in the oak grove of Mam're, the Amorite. And he lived like a sheikh of the desert, surrounded by the tents of his followers that were numbered now by hundreds.

Sitting at his door in the heat of the day, he offered hospitality to strangers, bidding them rest beneath the trees and refresh themselves with goat's milk poured from a goatskin bag, or with camel's milk, bread and dates. And Abraham and his son's sons who dwelt in such a manner, are called the patriarchs or fathers of their tribe.

And these were the days of the great Ham'mu-ra'bi, King of Babylon, an ally of the king of Elam; and it came to

Although no historical mention of Abraham is found in Egypt, Arthur Weigall, late Inspector-General of Antiquities for Egypt, says it is quite possible that Abraham's visit to that country was made just before the coming to the throne of Am'e-nem'het I, about 2111 B.C. when there was a mighty outcry from the people of Egypt because so many Semitic wanderers had come into the Delta, due to famine in their own land, that the country was overrun with their flocks and herds. As soon as Amenemhet came to the throne, he issued a decree driving the Asiatics from Egypt and built a wall to keep them out. This was perhaps why Abraham left Egypt.

pass that the kings of the plain fought with Hammurabi* and Ched'or-la-o'mer, King of Elam. Thus Lot was taken prisoner; but Abraham pursued the foe and rescued Lot and his people. Thereafter, the Dead Sea rose and covered Sodom and Gomorrah. Lot only escaped with his daughters, and Lot fled up to the mountains and dwelt there in a cave. Of Lot, so the Hebrews said, were descended their neighbors of Moab and Ammon.

And Abraham, then as always, clung to his vision of one God, one real and living God, one good God, and one only. And he heard in his heart, God's command: "Walk thou before me and be thou perfect." First of all men, Abraham recognized one God and a God that was perfect; first of all men, he saw the great hope that man might attain perfection. Though he himself often fell below that high ideal, it was he who first saw it for men, and from Abraham through Jesus, the line of spiritual growth was to be the increased understanding of what it meant to be perfect.

*Scholars believe that Amraphel of Shinar is Hammurabi, the great King of Babylon (2124-2081 B. C.), page 260.

The high place at Gezer as it is today.   All Semitic peoples worshipped at high places, and the Hebrew's vision of a purely spiritual religion was constantly being confused by the wanton customs, and cruel savagery connected with these high-places, where the material god of fertility and the earth mother under different names, were worshipped.   The stone pillars were symbols of the male god, and connected with them were the wooden pillars or "asherah," wrongly translated as "groves" in the Bible, the symbols of the female god or earth mother, Astarte, Ishtar, or Ashtoreth.   The hollow stone was either an altar or a laver, for the ceremonial washing of worshippers.

Now Abraham longed for a son to inherit the Land of Promise, and to carry on knowledge of the living God, which was to increase and unfold for generations to come. And Sarah bore him a son in her old age, and she cried aloud with joy: "God hath made me to laugh so that all that hear will laugh with me."

And the child was called Isaac, and he grew and was weaned and Abraham made a great feast the same day. And Abraham loved Isaac and centered his hopes on him; for Isaac was the old man's only heir, the only son of Sarah, his wife, sole hope of their old age.

A man standing in front of a sacred tree and two animals with their necks crossed, as the Canaanites themselves carved them on seals.   The wooden pillars of the high places were made as symbols of this tree, sacred to the earth mother, goddess of fertility.   (Found at Gezer.)

A jar containing a baby sacrificed at Gezer, and similar jars holding skeletons of infants found at Megiddo, evidence of the wide-spread custom in Canaan of sacrificing the first born son. A cemetery of jar-buried infants, none more than a week old, was found under the earth all over the high-place at Gezer. The babies were placed in large jars, and with them were buried smaller jars possibly with food for the use of the little victims in the world to come. Some of these skeletons showed marks of the sacrificial fire.

But Abraham looked on the Canaanites, and he saw how they offered their first born sons on the altars of their high-places. Then Abraham was confused and sorely tempted in mind. He yearned to be faithful and perfect and he thought that God required of him to sacrifice his son. So he rose up early one morning, and he saddled his ass, and took Isaac and two of his young men with him, and he clave the wood for the offering and went a three days' journey into the wilderness. Then he said unto his young men: "Abide ye here with the ass; while I and the lad go yonder."

And Abraham took the wood of the burnt offering and laid it upon Isaac his son; and he took the fire in his hand and a knife. And Isaac said: "My father, behold the fire and the wood, but where is the lamb for a burnt offering?"

And Abraham said: "My son, God will provide himself a lamb for a burnt offering."

And he built an altar and bound Isaac and laid him on the altar. Then he stretched forth his hand and took the knife to slay his son. But God stayed his hand and forbade him to sacrifice the lad. And Abraham saw a ram caught in a thicket, and he sacrificed that instead.

Isaac and Rebekah

Now Abraham would take no wife for Isaac from the Canaanites, lest the youth's budding vision of God should be blurred by a maiden of Canaanite customs. So Abraham sent his eldest servant to seek a wife for Isaac from the family of Na'hor, his brother. And the servant came unto Ha'ran at the time of the evening when women go forth to draw water; and he made his camels lie down by a well; and he prayed to be shown a damsel so kind that she would water his camels when he asked her for a drink.

And Rebekah came out, the granddaughter of Nahor, with her pitcher upon her shoulder. And the damsel was very fair, and she went down to the well, and the servant ran to meet her and asked her for a drink. And she let down her pitcher and gave him to drink; and she said: "I will draw for thy camels also." And she emptied her pitcher into the trough and drew for all the camels. And the man bowed his head and said: "Blessed be the God of Abraham."

Isaac leading Rebekah home to his mother's tent. The Hebrews at this period lived like wandering Arabs or Bedouins of today. Abraham, Isaac, and Jacob were great sheikhs of a single tribe. At the right are the black goat's hair tents of Abraham and Isaac. To the left appears a walled mud-brick town of the Canaanites.

And he went to the damsel's home and asked her father and mother to give her unto Isaac. And he gave the maid raiment and jewels. And they did eat and drink, he and the men that were with him. And Rebekah and her damsels rose up in the morning, and set themselves upon camels, and went their way with the servant.

And Isaac went out to meditate in the field at the eventide, and he lifted up his eyes, and behold the camels were coming. And Rebekah lighted off her camel, and took a veil and covered herself. And Isaac loved Rebekah, and brought her home to his tent.

Jacob Who Won the Name of Israel

Now unto Isaac and Rebekah were born twin sons, Jacob and Esau. And the boys grew, and Esau, the elder, was a hairy man and a cunning hunter, but Jacob was a plain man dwelling in tents.

And Esau took to wife two women of the Hittites, which was a grief of mind unto Isaac and Rebekah, and showed that through Esau true knowledge of God could not be carried on. And Isaac loved Esau; but Rebekah loved Jacob.

And when Isaac was old and his eyes were dim, he called Esau to him and bade him fetch him a mess of venison, promising to bless him, on his return, as coming chief of the tribe.

But while Esau went his way, Rebekah planned to trick Isaac. And she bade Jacob take a savory stew of kid's meat to his father, and she put the hairy skins of kids upon his hands and the smooth of his neck, that he might feel to Isaac's touch like Esau. Then she bade Jacob go in and say unto Isaac that he was Esau.

Thus Isaac, blindly groping, mistaking Jacob for Esau,

A group of Hittite demons, two with heads of lionesses and two with cloven hoofs,—a good reason why Rebekah did not care to have Jacob marry a maiden whose mind was full of such images. These demons were discovered in the important Hittite city of Car'che-mish. See pages 50, 97; also Vol. I, p. 228.

The sacrifice of a young lion before the Hittite god, Tesh'ub. Teshub, the figure with upraised axe at the left, appears to be taking a very lively part in the ceremony himself. A Hittite relief from Carchemish.

blessed his younger son as coming chief of the tribe; and Esau, returned from his hunting, found that he had been cheated of his birthright as eldest son. And he uttered a bitter cry and thought in his rage to slay Jacob.

And straightway, for her deceit, Rebekah feared for Jacob, and she said unto Isaac: "I am weary of my life because of the daughters of the Hittites. If Jacob take a wife from the Hittites, what good shall my life do me?"

And she begged Isaac to send Jacob back to Haran to get a wife from her kindred, thinking he would tarry there no more than a few short days till Esau's anger cooled; but when she said farewell to him, she said farewell forever; for he tarried twenty-one years.

And Jacob went his long way alone, and he slept by night on a pillow of stones; but even in fear and loneliness and consciousness of his guilt, he dreamt glorious dreams of promise, dreams of shining creatures mounting and descending a ladder to the skies, while the voice of God promised protection, promised that through him and his seed all the nations of earth should be blessed.

Then Jacob, the youth of visions, came to the well of Haran and beheld the shepherds there; and thither came Rachel, Rebekah's niece, with the flocks of La'ban, her father. And Jacob rolled away the stone from the mouth of the well that Rachel might water her sheep. And Jacob kissed Rachel. And Laban, hearing the tidings, ran and brought Jacob home.

Now Laban had two daughters. Leah the elder, was tender-eyed, but Rachel, the younger, was beautiful. And Jacob loved Rachel and he said unto Laban: "I will serve thee seven years for Rachel, thy younger daughter."

And Jacob served seven years for Rachel, tending the flocks and herds; and seven years seemed to him only a few short days for the love he had to Rachel. But when the time was fulfilled, Jacob found himself tricked, even as he had tricked Esau. For Laban gathered together all the men of the place to make the marriage feast, and he brought the bride in the evening, veiled, unto Jacob's tent, but in the morning, behold, the bride was Leah, not Rachel. And Jacob said unto Laban, "Wherefor hast thou beguiled me?"

And Laban answered, "It is not our custom here to give the younger daughter before the elder in marriage."

Then Jacob served seven years more, that he might win to him Rachel—for men in those days had many wives—and he took to wife, likewise, Bil'hah, the handmaid of Rachel, and Zil'pah, the handmaid of Leah.

And Jacob served other seven years for his share of Laban's flocks and herds, but he sore longed after his father's house; for Laban still found means to keep him from going home. And as he wandered by sunshine and starlight after his flocks in the pastures, the God of whom he had dreamed on the pillow of stones at Bethel, the God of his father Isaac, was very real to Jacob. And God said unto Jacob: "Get thee out from this land and return unto thy kindred."

Jacob's wives and children crossing the Jabbok by night. Background from an actual photograph of the Jabbok.

And Jacob rose up and set his sons and his wives upon camels, and he stole away unbeknown to Laban, fleeing with all his cattle and goods, for to go to Isaac, his father.

And he sent unto Esau messengers to say he was coming home; for he had heard that his brother, that wild, shaggy huntsman, Esau, dwelt in a fitting place mid the wild, jagged cliffs of Edom. And the messengers brought him word: "Thy brother cometh to meet thee and four hundred men come with him."

And there came a great fear upon Jacob, lest Esau intended to come and fall on his family, and slay them.

And Jacob halted by the brook Jab'bok, and he prayed unto God for deliverance. Then he sent unto Esau a present, 220 goats, 220 sheep, 30 camels with their colts, 50 cattle and 20 asses with their foals. And he sent his wives, his sons and his servants across the brook, and they forded the stream by night, the water ploughed by struggling beasts and gleaming under torches, with shrill cries of women and children above the noise of the beasts.

And when they had passed to the other side, Jacob was left alone with the river and the darkness. All night long he wrestled, alone with himself and God, struggling with fear and hatred, reckoning with the evil which he had done in the past. His old self resisted stiff-necked the angel of Love and goodness, that was striving to purify him. Mighty was the battle all through the hours of darkness. His future hung in the balance. But as the morning dawned, his stubborn resistance was broken, the power of God won the victory and the sun rose on Jacob changed in heart, cleansed of fear and hatred, strong in faith and love. And God said unto Jacob: "Thou shalt be called no more Jacob, but Israel (which means a Prince-that-has-power-with-God) for as a prince hast thou prevailed."

Henceforth the descendants of Jacob were called the Children of Israel, sons of him who wrestled with evil, fought a good fight and prevailed.

And Jacob lifted up his eyes and looked, and behold Esau came and with him four hundred men. And Jacob put himself at the head of his wives and children with Rachel, his best beloved, in the place of greatest safety, and he bowed to the ground seven times until he came near to his brother. But Esau ran to meet him and fell on his neck and kissed him. And they wept. And Esau greeted the women and children and said: "Wherefore sentest thou me the sheep and the goats, the camels, the cattle and the asses? I have enough, my brother."

But Jacob urged him and he took the gift, and they parted in very great kindness.

And Jacob journeyed to Canaan unto Isaac his father, and he builded altars unto the Lord and cleansed his house of idols.

The Babylonians had tales much like the Bible Tales of Creation and of the Flood, but they remained always a confused mixture of many fighting gods. In the Babylonian tale of Creation, all was chaos in the beginning as in Genesis, then the chief god Mar'duk overthrew Tia'mat, the demon of chaos, as light overcame darkness and chaos in the Bible. The picture above illustrates this conflict of Marduk with Tiamat, the demon. Rude carvings on seals found at Gezer illustrate this same story and show it was well-known in Palestine. Marduk next created land and sea, sun, moon and stars, animals and men. See page 31.

Doubtless Babylonians and Hebrews got their tales from the same original sources, but the way they were told in the two countries was very different indeed, the Hebrews rising slowly to the recognition of one God, a God who "looked on all he had made and behold it was very good;" the Chaldeans remaining always in the confused notion of many gods fighting with each other, jealous, vengeful, tricky, governing the universe in accordance with no universal law of goodness, but after their own ever changing passions and moods.

Now Jacob had twelve sons, and they dwelt in tents; and around the fires at eventide they told old tales of the flood and how the world was created, old, old tales of their people, some of which had been borrowed perhaps from their

Scholars see in the cylinder seal above, an illustration to some lost Babylonian tale resembling the story of Adam and Eve. A man and woman sit on either side of a tree, (perhaps the tree of life) and a serpent stands behind the woman, like the serpent who tempted Eve in the Bible. This second Creation story of the Bible (the Adam and Eve story told in Genesis II:4-III:24 and called by scholars the Jehovistic story because it uses Jehovah for the name of God), differs utterly from the first story told in Genesis I:1-II:4, which uses Elohim for the name of God, and tells nothing about the fall of man, but ends with the statement that God looked on all he had made and behold it was very good. Some scholars see in the tale of Adapa (p. 37) a likeness to the fall of Adam.

This picture shows the Babylonian conception of a tree of Life, guarded by two winged Cherubim, reminding one of the Bible Story of the Cherubim who were placed at the gate of the garden of Eden with a flaming sword to guard the way of the tree of Life (Gen. 3:24). It is taken from a marble slab found in a palace near Nineveh, and now in the British Museum. The Cherubim of the Bible, the glorious symbols of God's majesty and power, were doubtless conceived by the Hebrews from such sources as these. Sometimes the Cherubim of Babylon and Assyria had the heads of eagles, and they were akin to the colossal winged bulls and lions of the Babylonian palaces and temples, but always they were the impressive symbols of divine glory, majesty, and power. (See page 264.)

neighbors in far-off Chaldea, but were told in Jacob's tents with new and vital meaning, all having one single purpose—to show forth the power of God, and how He had chosen Abraham's seed, that they might carry the knowledge of Him to all the nations of earth.

The Babylonian Noah leaves the cabin of his Ark. Two gods stand on either side. Almost every nation has had some version of the flood story, even the distant Incas of Peru. Perhaps these wide-spread stories were echoes of an actual flood that swept the world when the glaciers melted in the days long before history. (See page 45.)

In the Babylonian tale which was found on clay tablets in the library of Assurbanipal at Nineveh, the hero is warned by one of the gods, that a flood is coming to destroy the world, and he is told just how to build a boat to escape it. He enters the boat with his wife and family and representatives of all kinds of beasts. When the flood abates, his boat goes aground on a mountain-top, as Noah's does in the Bible. He then sends out a dove to see if the waters have abated and the dove comes back having found no lighting place. He next sends out a swallow, but the swallow likewise returns. Lastly he sends out a raven, which does not return. So he knows the flood has abated. He lands with all living things and sacrifices to the gods. (See page 45.)

The main outline of this story is much like the Bible story of the Flood; but in spirit the two tales are utterly different. The Babylonian tale has no moral purpose. The flood is caused by one of the gods to punish evil-doers; but all the other gods oppose him, struggling, striving, quarreling and cowering like dogs, with fear. The Bible story on the other hand, holds aloft the conception of one God supreme in power, whose word is a law of purification to the world, wiping out evil and preserving only that which is nearest good.

Joseph and His Brethren
(ABOUT 1700 B.C.)

Now Israel loved Joseph more than all his children, because he was the son of Rachel, born in his old age, and Israel made Joseph a coat of many colors. But when Joseph's brethren saw that their father loved Rachel's son more than all the rest, they hated him and could not speak peaceably unto him.

And the brethren went to feed their father's flock in Shechem. And Israel said unto Joseph, "Go, I pray thee, and see whether it be well with them."

And when the brethren saw Joseph coming afar off, they conspired against him to slay him. And they stripped Joseph of his coat and cast him into a pit. And a company of Arabs came by with their camels, going down to Egypt with spicery, balm, and myrrh. And the brethren drew Joseph out of the pit, and sold him to the Arabs for twenty pieces of silver. And they killed a kid, and dipped Joseph's coat in the blood, and they brought the coat to their father and said, "This have we found."

And Israel said, "It is my son's coat. An evil beast hath devoured him."

And he rent his clothes, and mourned for his son many days.

Then the Arabs sold Joseph into Egypt unto Pot'i-phar, captain of Pharaoh's guard, and Potiphar made Joseph overseer over his house. But Potiphar's wife hated Joseph; and had him cast into prison.

Now Joseph found the King's butler and the King's baker in ward in the very same prison. And he told them the meaning of certain dreams which they dreamed. And things came to pass as Joseph had said. The king hanged the chief baker, but he restored the chief butler to his place. Yet did not the chief butler remember Joseph nor ask for his release.

And at the end of two full years Pharaoh dreamed a dream, and behold seven fat-fleshed kine came up out of the river, and behold seven other kine, lean and ill-favored, came out of the river after them, and ate the fat-fleshed kine. And Pharaoh was troubled and sent for his wise-men, but none could interpret his dream. Then the butler remembered to speak of Joseph and Pharaoh sent servants to fetch him.

And Joseph shaved himself and changed his raiment and came in unto Pharaoh. And Pharaoh said to Joseph, "I have heard say of thee, that thou canst interpret a dream."

And Joseph answered, saying: "It is not in me to interpret your dream. God shall give Pharaoh an answer."

And Pharaoh told Joseph his dream, and Joseph said: "The seven good kine are seven good years, and the seven lean kine are seven years of famine. Behold, there come seven years of great plenty throughout the land of Egypt, and after them seven years of famine. Now therefore, let Pharaoh look out a man discreet and wise and set him over the land of Egypt. And let them gather all the food of those good years for a store against the years of famine."

And the thing was good in Pharaoh's eyes. And he said unto Joseph: "There is none so wise as thou art. Be thou over my house." And he arrayed Joseph in fine linen and put a gold chain about his neck, and made him to ride in his second chariot, and servants cried: "Bow the knee!"

And in the seven plentiful years, Joseph laid up food, till there came the years of dearth on all the lands but Egypt.

Then Jacob must needs send Joseph's brethren down to buy corn in Egypt,—all save the young lad, Benjamin; for

Joseph becomes a great man in Egypt. No positive record of Joseph has been found in Egypt, but a very ancient canal is still called by the Egyptians Joseph's Canal, (Bahr Yusuf) suggesting that memories of Joseph still linger in Egyptian tradition.

Rachel had died when he was born, and now that Joseph was gone, Jacob loved Benjamin more than all his sons.

And the brothers bowed down before Joseph, although they knew him not. And Joseph's heart was full. Nevertheless, he spake roughly: "Ye are spies. Take home the corn; but one of you shall stay bound, till ye bring me this youngest brother whom you have left at home!"

Then the brethren cried out in sore distress: "This evil is come upon us because of our guilt toward Joseph."

And Joseph wept in secret, yet he kept Simeon bound.

And the brethren went and told Jacob and Jacob said: "My son, Benjamin, shall never go to Egypt."

But the famine was sore in the land, and when they had eaten the corn, Judah made solemn promise to guard the lad with his life; so Jacob at last let him go.

And Joseph's heart yearned upon Benjamin as he looked on the face of the lad, and he entered his chamber and wept. Then he washed his face and went out and ordered a feast.

Semites, like Joseph's brethren, prisoners in Egypt. From a tomb carving (Leyden Museum). The men are manacled with wooden manacles and all are led by Egyptian soldiers. The woman at the rear carries two babies at her back.

And when his brethren had eaten, he sent them away with sacks full of corn; but he bade his steward secretly return to each sack the money paid, and hide in Benjamin's sack a beautiful silver cup; for he had it in mind to try his brothers to see if their hearts had changed.

And the steward followed the brethren and halted them on the road, crying that they were thieves. And he searched the sacks and found their coins, and when he came on the silver cup hidden in Benjamin's sack, he seized the lad and

Jacob and his sons coming into Egypt with their wives and children. Costumes drawn from a tomb painting. Semites now wear long strips of bright colored wool wound around their bodies. Women carry babies in slings.

dragged him away, as if to take him to prison. Then the brethren rent their clothes and returned again to the city.

And Judah said unto Joseph: "We have a father, my lord, an old man, and Benjamin is the child of his old age, a little one, and his father loveth him. If we return without the lad, our father will die. Now therefore, I pray thee, let me abide instead of Benjamin, a bondman unto my lord."

And Joseph, beholding how tender love had replaced the sullen envy that had darkened the hearts of his brethren, fell on the neck of Benjamin, forgave them all and kissed them. And he bade them return to Canaan and bring their father and all their goods, to settle near him in Egypt.

So they took their wives and little ones, their cattle and household goods, and came again into Egypt.

And Joseph made ready his chariot and went up to meet his father, and he fell on his neck and wept. And Pharaoh gave Joseph's brethren the greenest pasture-lands in the flat, rich fields of Go'shen.

And afterwards the Hyk'-sos, Asiatic herdsmen, akin to the Children of Israel, came and conquered Egypt. And Israel prospered under their rule, and grew from a family into a nation; for the children of Jacob's twelve sons became the twelve tribes of Israel.

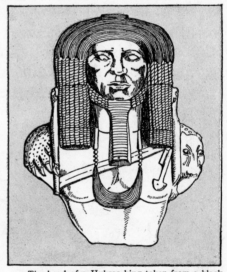

The head of a Hyksos king taken from a black granite statue found in Egypt. The Hyksos, or Shepherd kings, were invaders of Egypt, a mixed multitude of warlike tribes akin to the Israelites. They were hard-featured warriors, with broad faces, high cheek bones, flat noses, and mouths curved sternly downward.

The king in this picture wears barbaric ornaments, a heavy plaited wig, and a natural beard like the Israelites but quite unlike the Egyptians who had clean-shaven faces. To this he has made the ridiculous addition of a second beard, the false beard of Egyptian Pharaohs.

Under him, and his successors, the descendants of Jacob prospered, and grew from a tribe to a nation. The twelve tribes of Israel were Reu'ben, Sim'e-on, Le'vi, Ju'dah, Is'sa-char, Zeb'u-lun, Benjamin, Dan, Naph'ta-li, Gad, Ash'er, and two half tribes, E'phra-im and Ma-nas'seh descended from Joseph's sons.

V

Moses and the Conquest of Canaan
Going Forth Out of Egypt
(ABOUT 1230 B. C.)

Now it chanced that the children of Israel dwelt for four hundred years in Egypt; but during that time Egyptian princes, subject Kings of Thebes, drove out the Hyksos or Shepherd kings, who were akin to the Hebrews, and there came to rule over Egypt a new and forceful line which knew not Joseph,—Thut'mose III, who conquered Canaan and Syria; Akh-na'ton the thinker, with his mighty dream of world peace, for which the world was unready; Seti I and Ram'ses II, his son, who set out to win back the empire lost by Akhnaton. And Ramses feared all that foreign race,

This picture shows why Seti I and his son Ramses II constantly feared lest the Israelites in their midst should join themselves to Egypt's enemies. Seti is shown conquering a Canaanite stronghold belonging to Semites of race akin to Israel.

The great conqueror Thutmose III had subdued Canaan and Syria and made them subject to Egypt (Vol. I, 181), but in the days of the dreamer Akhnaton these provinces fell away and became part of the Hittite Empire (Vol. I. 216) When Akhnaton's line died out, Seti I set out boldly to recover the coveted provinces and Ramses II, his son, followed his father's example, constantly warring with Israel's cousins in Canaan (Vol. I, 226).

Seti gallops alone into battle, riding over the bodies of the Semites who are clad in leather armor with strips of leather bound tightly around the upper part of their bodies. Seti is painted of enormous size to dwarf the importance of his foes. In the upper left corner a typical Canaanite stronghold on a rocky hill, falls before his attack and the defenders break their bows in token of surrender. A carving from the temple of Amon at Karnak.

which had waxed so rich and so mighty in the midst of the land of Egypt. And he said unto his people: "Behold, the Children of Israel are more and mightier than we. Come on, let us deal wisely with them lest they multiply and it come to pass that, when there falleth out any war, they join also unto our enemies and fight against us."

Therefore he set over them taskmasters to afflict them. And they built for Pharaoh treasure cities, Pi'thom and Ra-am'ses; and the Egyptians made the Children of Israel to serve with rigor. And they made their lives bitter with hard bondage in mortar and in brick, and in all manner of service in the field.

A statue now in the Turin Museum of Ramses II (1296-1225 B.C.), who has long been regarded as the Pharaoh of the oppression of Israel. Ramses followed his father's example subduing the Asiatics.

And Pharaoh charged all his people saying, "Every son that is born to the Israelites, ye shall cast into the river."

Now there was born a son unto Am'ram and Joch'e-bed of the tribe of Levi. And Jochebed saw that her son was a goodly child, and she hid him three months in the house, and when she could no longer hide him, she put him in a basket of papyrus reeds and laid it in the flags by the river. And his sister stood afar off to watch what would be done unto him.

And the daughter of Pharaoh came down to wash herself at the river; and her maidens walked along by the river's side; and she saw the basket among the flags, and sent her maid to fetch it. And when she had opened it, she saw the child, and behold the babe wept. And she had compassion on him and said: "This is one of the Hebrew's children."

Then said his sister to Pharaoh's daughter: "Shall I call

a Hebrew woman that she may nurse the child for thee?"

And Pharaoh's daughter said, "Go."

And the maid went and called the child's mother; and Pharaoh's daughter said: "Nurse this child for me."

And Jochebed took the child home. And she sang him the songs of his father's God, the God of Abraham, Isaac and Jacob; and the child grew and his mother brought him unto Pharaoh's daughter and he became her son. And she called his name Moses, and he was brought up in a palace, and learned in all the wisdom of the Egyptians.

But it came to pass when he was grown, that he went out unto the Israelites, and looked upon their burdens. And he spied an Egyptian smiting an Hebrew, and his Hebrew blood boiled within him. And he slew the Egyptian and

The Hebrew slaves working in the Egyptian brick yards must have looked like this. This picture is painted on the walls of a tomb and represents Syrian and Phoenician slaves, Semites like the Hebrews, at work in a brickyard of Thutmose III. In the upper picture at the left, a man is emptying a bucket of mud while a taskmaster, holding a rod, sits by and watches him. Two men carry loads of bricks with yokes and cords. Another taskmaster with rod threateningly extended, watches two men carrying mud in vessels on their shoulders, while a third with yoke and cords returns for another load. The inscription in hieroglyphics at the top of the picture announces that the taskmaster says to the laborers: "The rod is in my hand; be not idle!"

Below at the left is a pond surrounded by trees and filled with water lilies. One man stands in the pond; the other leans over toward it, both bringing water for the work. In the center a group of men cut off portions of soft clay while one carries it in a bucket on his shoulder to the moulder at the right above. The moulder pushes the clay into an oblong box which is the mould. He has already finished three bricks. In the center, near the pond, a moulder spreads out the soft bricks with spaces between for the circulation of air to make them dry quickly in the sun.

The ruins of the store-chambers for grain and provisions in the treasure city of Pithom were excavated by Naville in 1883 and he found there at the corners of the brickwork, bricks made without straw, just as the Bible had said. Pharaoh made the Israelites make bricks without straw, because straw held the clay together and to make them without straw was a far more laborious task. Pithom was built by Ramses II to serve as a base of supplies for his armies in Asia and was strongly fortified. The treasure-cities were really fortified granaries.

Moses, in his Egyptian dress, looks on the burdens of the Israelites.   The great temples and colossal statues of the Egyptians were raised at tremendous cost in labor, with the sweat and agony of multitudes of whip-driven slaves. In an original Egyptian picture of slaves dragging a colossal statue, 172 men are needed, four rows of 43 each.

hid him in the sand. And he chose rather to suffer afflic-tion with the people of God, than to enjoy the pleasures of Egypt.

And the next day he saw two Hebrews striving together, and he said unto him that did the wrong: "Wherefore smitest thou thy fellow?"

But the Hebrews had grown sullen through slavery and sorrow, and this one mocked and said: "Who made thee a judge over us? Intendest thou to kill me as thou killedst the Egyptian?"

And Moses saw that his crime was known, and he fled to Mid'i-an in the Si'nai wilderness. And he sat down by a well.

Now Jeth'ro, the priest of Midian, had seven daughters, and they came and drew water and filled the troughs to water their father's flocks. And the shepherds drove them away; but Moses drove off the shepherds and watered the flocks for the maidens. Then Jethro gave Moses his daughter Zip'po-rah to wife; and Moses dwelt in Midian keeping the flocks of Jethro. And in the lone stretches of wilderness, his passionate anger cooled, and he said again in his heart:

"Lord, thou hast been our dwelling place
     in all generations;
Before the mountains were brought forth,
Or ever thou hadst formed the earth and the world,
Even from everlasting to everlasting thou art God."

And it came to pass in process of time that the king of Egypt died and Mer-ne'ptah, his son, became Pharaoh.

A statuette inscribed with the name of Moses in very ancient Hebrew script, possibly a likeness of Moses. When Moses first came to the Sinai peninsula, still beardless and partly Egyptian in customs, it is quite possible he worked with other Semitic laborers in the Egyptian copper mines in Sinai, where the Egyptians had colonies of miners for many generations. See Vol. I, pp. 85, 93.

This statue was found by Professor Flinders Petrie while excavating an Egyptian temple at the base of Mt. Sinai, and with it were eight tablets written in a script which Mr. Petrie could not read. Scholars of England, France and Germany studied these tablets and now it is announced by Professor Hugo Grimme of the University of Munster, Germany, that the script is a very ancient form of Hebrew; that it has all been translated and that the letters near the base of the statue say "Moses."

And the Children of Israel groaned by reason of the bondage. And Moses led his flocks to the backside of the desert and came unto Mt. Sinai.

And the Lord appeared unto Moses in a flame of fire out of the midst of a bush. And God said: "I am come to deliver my people and bring them unto a good land, flowing with milk and honey, unto the place of the Canaanites, and the Hittites, and the Amorites. Come now, I will send thee to Pharaoh."

And Moses said, "Who am I that I should go to Pharaoh?"

And God said, "Certainly I will be with thee."

And Moses said, "O my Lord, but I am slow of speech."

But the Lord said: "Aar'on, thy brother, speaks well. He shall be thy spokesman and I will teach thee what to do."

And Moses took his wife and his sons and set them upon an ass and returned to the land of Egypt.

And Moses and Aaron gathered together all the elders of Israel and told them that the Lord would lead them back to Canaan, whence their fathers had come in the days of Jacob and Joseph. And they went and said unto Pharaoh: "Thus saith the Lord God of Israel, Let my people go that they may hold a feast unto me."

The upper part of the famous triumph tablet of Merneptah, found by Professor Petrie at Thebes in 1896, and containing the first mention of Israel known in Egyptian monuments. Relating all his triumphs, Merneptah says on this stone "Plundered is Canaan; ... Israel is desolated, her seed is not; Palestine has become a defenseless widow because of Egypt." This shows that Israel was already in Palestine and so well established there as to be referred to as a nation in the days of Merneptah, which would make it seem probable that the Israelites in Egypt were only a small tribe of a race already settled in Palestine, unless the Exodus took place before the time of Merneptah. Further investigation may prove the Exodus to have been earlier.

And Pharaoh said: "Who is the Lord that I should obey His voice? I know not the Lord, neither will I let Israel go."

And Pharaoh commanded the taskmasters, saying, "Lay more work on these Israelites; for they be idle, they be idle! Therefore they cry: 'Let us go and sacrifice to our God.'"

And the Children of Israel groaned and said unto Moses: "Why didst thou not let us alone? Thou hast made us to suffer the more."

But Aaron, at God's command, lifted up his rod and smote the waters of the Nile in the sight of Pharaoh and his servants. And there fell ten plagues on Egypt. And the fish in the rivers died; and the people saw how the Nile, their own great river Nile, which they had thought was a god, giving life to all the land, could not protect itself, nor keep the fish alive. The rivers which they worshipped

A group of Egyptian Gods, to prove the powerlessness of which the wonders of Moses were wrought.   Nehebka, the serpent goddess; Sekhmet, the lioness-headed; Sebek, the crocodile-god; Isis with the head of a cow, and Horus with the head of a hawk.

brought forth a plague of frogs; the dust of the earth turned to lice; the air brought forth flies; the beasts which they needed for sacrifice were smitten with disease.

The gods of Egypt were powerless to stop the plague of boils that broke forth on man and beast, the fierce rain of hail that brake every tree of the field, and the fearful cloud of locusts that covered the face of the earth and ate up every green thing. Even the sun-god Rä, the greatest of all Egyptian gods, whose brilliance filled the land, was hidden three days by darkness.

Now Pharaoh called the magicians to copy the wonders of Moses by means of tricks and enchantments; but after the second plague they could no more imitate him. The gods of Egypt stood revealed as powerless creations of fancy, the source of plagues, not blessings.

Whenever the suffering was most intense, Pharaoh would summon Moses and say that the Hebrews might go; but when the suffering was over, Pharaoh recalled his promise, till Moses cried in anger, "At midnight all the first born sons in the land of Egypt shall die."

Then the Hebrews made ready to go. Standing with staff in hand, loins girded and shoes on their feet, they ate a last meal in haste, roast lamb with unleavened bread; for they could not tarry till their dough should rise, but bound up their kneading troughs in the bundle of clothes on their shoulders. And the meal was called the Passover, because the Lord passed over the houses of the Hebrews and saved them from the plagues when the houses of Egypt were smitten. Therefore did the Children of Israel, from that day forward, celebrate yearly the Passover.

And at midnight the first born son in each house in Egypt died, and there rose a great cry in the land.

And Pharaoh called Moses and Aaron and said: "Get thee forth from among my people."

The Israelites crossing the Red Sea.   Background sketched from a photograph taken at one of the shallow spots where wind and tide today might blow the water aside and for a short time leave dry land, were it not for the Suez Canal and the protection of its earth works.

And the Children of Israel left in the darkness of early dawn; they journeyed from Raamses to Suc'coth, 600,000 on foot, men, women and children with flocks and herds.

But Pharaoh took six hundred chariots and his horsemen and all his army, and pursued the Children of Israel even to the Red Sea. And the Children of Israel lifted their eyes and behold, the Egyptians marched after them! And they were sore afraid and complained again unto Moses: "Why hast thou led us away to die? It were better to serve the Egyptians."

But Moses answered with patience: "Fear ye not. Stand still and see the salvation of the Lord which He will show to you today; for the Egyptians whom ye have seen today, ye shall see them again no more forever."

And Moses stretched out his hand over the sea, and the Lord caused the sea to go back by a strong east wind all that night and the waters were divided. And the Children of Israel went into the midst of the sea upon the dry land; and the waters were a wall unto them on their right hand and on their left. And the Egyptians went in after them, even all Pharaoh's horses, his chariots and his horsemen.

And Moses stretched forth his hand and the sea returned to his strength when the morning appeared and the Egyptians fled against it. And the Lord overthrew the Egyptians in the midst of the sea. And the waters covered the chariots and all the host of Pharaoh.

Then the Children of Israel sang a song of triumph; for God seemed to them a God of war, because they saw His power overcoming the boasts of evil, breaking the chains of the tyrant, and setting the captives free. And they sang:

> "I will sing unto the Lord;
> For He hath triumphed gloriously;
> The horse and his rider
> Hath He thrown into the sea!"

And Mir'i-am, the sister of Moses, took a timbrel in her hand, and all the women went after her with timbrels and with dances; and they answered each other, singing.

So the Children of Israel journeyed from the Red Sea through the wilderness; but their noisy rejoicing died when they grew hungry and thirsty; for they still had the hearts of slaves. And they wailed and said: "We remember the fish we did eat in Egypt freely, the cucumbers and the melons, the leeks, the onions and the garlic. Would to God we had died in Egypt when we sat by the flesh pots and when we ate bread to the full; for ye have brought us into this wilderness to kill us all with hunger."

And they were ready to stone Moses. But Moses cried unto God; and he guided the people to Elim, an oasis in the desert, where were twelve wells of cool water, and three score and ten green palm trees. And they encamped there by the waters. And when they went forth again, quails and manna appeared to feed the murmuring people.

And in the third month, they pitched their tents beneath the tall mass of Mount Sinai. And the glory of the Lord abode upon the Mount, like to devouring fire. And there were thunders and lightnings and a cloud upon the Mount. And the Lord called Moses to the top of the Mount and said: "I am the Lord thy God, which have brought thee out of the land of Egypt, out of the house of bondage,

Thou shalt have no other gods before me;
Thou shalt not make unto thee any graven image;
Thou shalt not take the name of the Lord thy God in vain;
Remember the Sabbath Day to keep it holy;
Honour thy father and thy mother;
Thou shalt not kill;
Thou shalt not commit adultery;
Thou shalt not steal;
Thou shalt not bear false witness;
Thou shalt not covet."

The majestic mass of Mt. Sinai sketched from a photograph. Near here Moses kept the flocks of Jethro his father-in-law. Near here he saw the vision of the flaming bush that led him back to deliver his people from Egypt.

Standing on this mountain top, deeply uplifted in spirit and inspired as are all great men who sincerely yearn for truth, he received the Ten Commandments which have been the moral law of the Christian and Hebrew world.

It was from Moses that the Israelites received the name of Jehovah or "Yahveh," for God. As time passed, they regarded the name as too sacred even to speak. It was written Y H V H with no vowels.

And all the people saw the lightnings and the mountain smoking and they heard the thundering and the voice of the trumpet exceeding loud, and they trembled and stood afar off.

And the Lord called Moses again, and Moses took with him Joshua, the Chief of the fighting men. And he left Aaron and Hur in charge of the people, and went into the midst of the cloud that burned with fiery glory; and he was on the mount forty days and forty nights. And Joshua awaited him at the foot of the mount below.

And when the people saw that Moses delayed to come down they gathered themselves unto Aaron and said, "Up!

Make us gods; for as for this man Moses, we know not what is become of him."

And Aaron bade the people bring him their earrings; and he fashioned the gold with a graving tool and made them a golden calf.

And all the people looked on the calf and said: "These be thy gods, O Israel, which brought thee up out of Egypt."

And Aaron built an altar before the calf, and the people rose early on the morrow and offered burnt offerings before it. And they sat down to eat and drink and rose up to play.

And Moses came down from the Mount bearing the Ten Commandments inscribed on two tables of stone. And Joshua heard the noise of the people as they shouted and he said: "I hear the noise of them that sing."

And it came to pass as they two drew nigh unto the

Moses and Joshua, returning from Mt. Sinai, find the people worshipping the golden calf. Joshua, the young warrior, had lately been appointed Captain of the Host, and had already fought at least one battle with wandering Am'a-lek-ites, Bedouins of the desert. (Exodus 17:8-16). Moses took Joshua as his sole companion and left him at the base of Mt. Sinai when he himself went to the summit to receive the Ten Commandments. Joshua was his companion when he returned to meet this great disappointment in the faithlessness of his people.

Joshua's leather armor is copied from that of Semitic warriors in the army of Egypt, as depicted on tombs of the period. (See pages 116 and 140.) Moses' costume is from Egyptian tomb paintings. The golden calf is taken from a calf-vessel modelled by Israelites and found in a tomb at Gezer. The background of the picture is from a photograph of the hill of Aaron's Calf, near Mt. Sinai.

camp that they saw the golden calf and the people dancing naked.

And Moses' anger waxed hot and he cast the tables out of his hand and brake them beneath the Mount. And he took the calf and burnt it in the fire and ground it to powder and strewed it upon the water and made the Children of Israel drink of it. And he rebuked Aaron sternly and cried in the gate of the camp: "Who is on the Lord's side, come unto me."

And all the sons of Levi gathered themselves unto him and they slew of the rebellious Children of Israel 3,000 men that day. But the heart of Moses was sore for the love he still bare his people. And he cried out unto God: "O Lord, this people have sinned a great sin, yet now forgive their sin,"—his voice failed for fulness of grief—"if Thou canst not forgive them, I pray Thee, blot me out of Thy book."

But the Lord said unto Moses: "Hew thee two tables of stone like unto the first and come up again to the Mount."

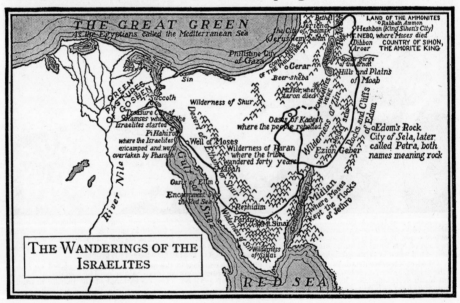

THE WANDERINGS OF THE ISRAELITES

The Ark of the Covenant held the stone tablets, engraved with the Ten Commandments.

The Ark was a wooden box overlaid with gold, three and three-fourths feet long by two and a half feet wide, and two and a fourth feet high. It was surrounded at the top by a crown or raised ornament of gold; and the pure gold lid, which was called the Mercy Seat, was surmounted by two golden cherubim facing each other, and spreading their wings so they touched, to guard the Mercy Seat; for the Mercy Seat always represented to the Hebrews the presence of God among them.

The Ark had four rings at the four corners, through which could be slipped the wooden staves by which it was carried on the march. It was regarded as so sacred that none but the High Priest ever looked upon it and when the Israelites were on the march, it was covered from sight by a blue veil.

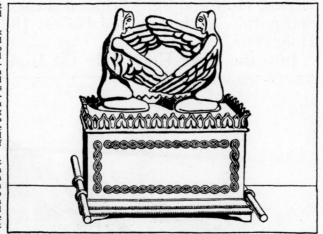

And Moses went up Mount Sinai, and received again the tables engraved with the Ten Commandments.

Then Moses bade the people make an ark to hold the tables of the covenant. And they made a box of acacia wood overlaid with gold; and two golden figures of cherubim, spreading their wings on high, covered the golden lid which was called the Mercy Seat.

And Moses bade the people build a great tent or tabernacle and put the ark in its Holiest Place, that they might have the Commandments where the nations round about would have placed some grotesque stone image to represent their god.

And the people gave their jewels, bracelets and earrings of gold, and they willingly wrought and spun until they had made a splendid tent, having curtains of fine twined linen in blue and purple and scarlet; and they stretched out over these a covering of goat's hair with one of ramskin dyed red, and one of thick badger skins, to make a complete protection in case of stormy weather.

And they placed the Ark of the Covenant within the

Holiest Holy and hung before it a curtain of scarlet, blue and purple, to shut off the Holiest Holy from the outer Holy Place.

Into the Inner Holy, only the High Priest might go,

The tabernacle as it appeared in the wilderness. The lower part of the tabernacle, to the south, west and north was made of boards fastened together with rings through which bars could be slipped so it might easily be taken to pieces; for the tabernacle was taken down and carried about whenever the Israelites changed their camp.

The great tent was covered first with curtains of fine twined linen, blue and purple and scarlet, embroidered with figures of cherubim. Over this to serve as a complete protection in stormy weather, were three more sets of curtains, one of goat's hair, one of ramskins, dyed red and one of badger skins. To the east, which was the entrance, were five pillars overlaid with gold and bearing hangings of fine linen.

Inside the Tabernacle were only the small Holy of Holies, where stood the Ark and the Outer Holy Place, where stood the altar of incense, the table of show-bread, and the seven branched candlestick. These two divisions of the tabernacle were separated by the veil, a curtain of blue, purple and scarlet, embroidered with cherubim. The tabernacle stood in a great court—150x75 ft. in size. This court was enclosed by canvas curtains, 7½ ft. high, making a continuous wall except for the embroidered curtains of entrance at the east. Only into this court did the people themselves dare to come.

The altar on which offerings were burnt stood inside the court and just before the door of the Tabernacle. It was overlaid with brass and had a brazen horn at each of the four corners. Between it and the Tabernacle was the laver for the priests. (See page 134.)

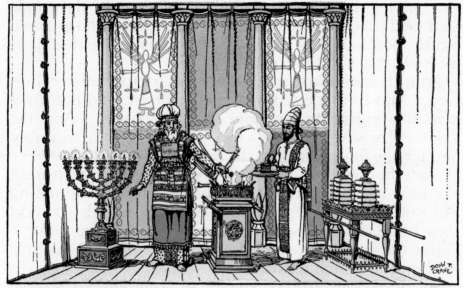

To the left is the High Priest in his long blue robe, edged with pomegranates and little golden bells, that tinkled as he walked.   He wears his ephod or sacred coat of gold, blue, purple and scarlet, held at the shoulders with onyx-stones engraved with the names of the twelve tribes of Israel.   On his breast he wears the breast plate set with Urim and Thummin, twelve shining jewels each engraved with the name of one of the tribes of Israel.   On his head is his mitre, bearing in front a gold plate with the words "Holiness to the Lord."

To the right is a common priest in white.   Both are barefoot and they are standing in the Holy Place of the Tabernacle. Behind them is the veil or curtain which shuts off the Holiest Holy and hides the Ark of the Covenant. Between them is the Golden altar of incense, the symbol of prayer; to the left is the seven-branched golden candle-stick, the sign of God as the light of Israel; to the right is the table of showbread, the sign of close communion with God and acknowledgment of God as the very life of Israel.

The golden candlestick pictured here is taken from the actual candlestick as engraved on the arch of Titus in Rome.   It was not a candlestick, but held seven richly adorned lamps and was lighted every evening and dressed every morning.   The table of showbread held twelve loaves of unleavened bread, representing the twelve tribes of Israel.   Every Sabbath, new baked loaves were put on the table in two rows of six each.

and he but once a year as into the presence of God.   Into the Outer Holy the priests came once a day to renew the oil and the incense; but the people themselves drew no nearer the tent than an outer court of assembly, where they watched the priests burn offerings on the altar of sacrifice; for God still seemed to the common people very far out of their reach, wrapt in awful majesty, as in the thunders of Sinai. Not till twelve hundred years later was Jesus the Christ to teach them to find God very near, speaking to each in the still small voice within his own heart and soul.

Thus Moses drew his people together into a unified nation

through regular worship of God, and he taught the people that God was the one and only God, the God who guarded Israel, of whom they could make no image, because he is life itself, Jehovah the great "I am."

And Moses set the tribe of Levi apart to minister unto God. And he made Aaron the High Priest, and put upon him holy garments for glory and for beauty. And the Levites blew silver trumpets for the calling of the assembly and for the journeyings of the camp.

And the Children of Israel marched from Horeb unto Ka'desh, a green and fertile oasis, beneath the gleaming white of a wall of limestone hills. And Moses said: "Beyond these hills lieth the Promised Land; go ye up and possess it."

But the people were afraid and they said, "Let us first send men to search out the land."

So Moses sent Joshua, the son of Nun, and Ca'leb, the son of Je-phun'neh, with ten other fighting men to spy out the Land of Canaan, and they went up beyond the hills and entered into Canaan; and there they saw the strong walled towns that crowned the towering hill-tops; and they saw the Children of Anak, ancient natives of the land, so tall that they seemed like giants. And they took of the pomegranates and figs and they bare a cluster of grapes between them upon a staff and they hasted back unto Moses, saying:

"Surely, the land floweth with milk and honey and this is the fruit of it. Nevertheless the people be strong that dwell in the land, and the cities are walled up to heaven."

And all the congregation lifted up their voices and wept. But Caleb attempted to still them, saying; "Let us go at once and possess the land; for we are well able to overcome it."

Nevertheless the spies that went with him said, "We be not able to overcome it; for the people are stronger than we. There we saw the giants, the sons of Anak; we were in our own sight as grasshoppers, and so we were in their sight!"

A fortified town on a hill, typical scenery in Palestine as the Hebrews first saw it. The rocky hillsides of creamy stone, terraced on the lower slopes in little green patches of fields and vineyards, contrasted strongly with the perfectly flat green fields which they had left behind in Egypt. Figures of the giants are from the Canaanite warriors, on page 386.

According to James Baikie in "Lands and Peoples of the Bible," enormous caves have been discovered all over southern Palestine which give every indication of having been lived in by a very large race of men. He says (page 60) "The sons of Anak, the Emim, or Dreadful Ones, the Zamzummim or Stammerers, the Rephaim and Nephilim (giants), all these, by whatever name they were called were no fantastic dream of the early Hebrew invaders. A race of big men there was, big enough to frighten the Hebrews at all events, and here and there, no doubt, as among all tall races, an extra big fellow like Goliath; and they hewed for themselves those great caves."

And all the Children of Israel murmured and said: "Let us make a captain and return again to Egypt."

Then Moses and Aaron fell on their faces, and Joshua and Caleb rent their clothes and said: "But the land is a good land; and the Lord will bring us into it. Rebel not ye against the Lord, neither fear ye the people of the land."

But the people bade stone them with stones.

And the Lord said unto Moses, "Get you into the wilderness. Forty years shall this people wander; all that are today over twenty years of age, saving only Caleb and Josh'u-a, shall die. They shall not see the Promised Land which they have despised, but their little ones shall possess it."

And when Moses told the people all that the Lord had said, they mourned and rose up early and said, "Now we will obey and go over those hills and possess the Promised Land."

But Moses said, "It is too late. Ye should have obeyed at first. The Lord is no more with you."

Nevertheless, they presumed to go up in the wilfulness of their hearts, and the Canaanites which dwelt in that hill smote them and chased them even as bees do and drove them down the mount. And the Children of Israel turned about and wandered in the wilderness.

Entering the Promised Land

Now it came to pass after forty years that the Children of Israel came again to the cavernous mountains of E'dom,

And Edom was the "Red Land," a land of towering rocks with jagged peaks and pinnacles, that glowed like molten copper when kindled to life by the sun.

The Israelites encamped by tribes and shut off from the Promised Land only by a range of granite hills. Background copied from a photograph of an oasis in the Sinai Desert.

The brilliant rock city of Sela or Petra as it was in the days of Moses, a city naturally fortified by its towering walls of cliffs, back of which on every side lay the sands of the Arabian Desert. The only entrance into this ancient stronghold of Edom, was through the Sik or Gorge, a cool and gloomy canyon, with sides three hundred feet high, and walls that projected in places, and often nearly met above the traveler's head.

Having journeyed a mile and a half up this narrow, twisting defile, the traveler all at once saw a glorious rock-hewn city bursting upon his view, great walls of natural rock, gleaming rose and lilac, salmon, crimson, sunset-hued; and into this rainbow colored rock, men had carved temples and tombs, stairways, roads and dwellings, while down below in the circle enclosed by these towering walls, houses and public buildings stood, lining the thread of a stream.

Sela was once a great city, splendid, powerful and wealthy. Kings, queens, conquerors, marveled at its beauty. Rich caravans filed up its entrance gorge, and then for 1300 years, it lay deserted and hidden, known only to wandering Arabs. So it was until 1812, when travelers again discovered it; and now once again today travellers sufficiently adventurous may visit its glorious ruins and dream of Moses and Joshua. (See the maps on pages 128 and 146.)

The ruins of the rock-hewn road to the high place at Sela and the guardian pillars of rock as they are today. The word Sela in Hebrew means rock. Later the city was called Petra, the Greek word for rock. Legends of Moses still cling to the place. According to Arab tradition, it was near this place that Moses struck the rock, when water gushed forth for his people. The valley is still called Valley of Moses, and almost every Arab tent has a child named Moses. The editor visited this city and climbed up this road to the high place.

In the heart of that brilliant mass lay the famous rock city of Se-la, approached through a narrow gorge; a hidden mountain stronghold, surrounded by walls of cliffs into which dwellings were cut, with tombs and roads and stairways hewn in the solid rock, and a high place over all where the Edomites worshipped their god. The kings of Edom had conquered the original Ho'rite cave-dwellers, and carved out that rocky stronghold while the Hebrews were still in Egypt.

And Moses sent messengers unto the King of Edom, saying, "Let us pass, I pray thee, through thy country. We will not trample the fields or the vineyards. We will go by the king's highway. And if our cattle drink of thy water, we will pay thee for it."

But the King of Edom said, "Thou shalt not go through;" and he came with much people, and a strong hand out of Sela, his stronghold.

Nevertheless, the Children of Israel would make no war upon Edom; for the Edomites were their kindred, descended from Esau, Isaac's son. Instead, they turned about and skirted the cliffs of Edom till they came to the high, breezy table-land that forms the plains of Moab, a land of hay and green things with shouting in the busy fields and singing in the vineyards, a land of grapes and summer fruit and brooklets edged with willows.

And the Moabites and wild Ammonites who dwelt still further northward, were descendants of Abraham's nephew, Lot, and spoke, with little difference, the very same Hebrew tongue.

The plains of Moab with the ancient town of Madeba reconstructed from its ruins. One can still stand on the mound and look for ten miles about without seeing a sign of a bush or tree about the waving grain. Although there were mountains in Moab, the country was chiefly renowned for its high-lying wheat-covered plains, contrasting very sharply with the wild, rocky cliffs of Edom, where fertile land was hard to find, and only a few rich valleys produced some grapes or grain. It was near this spot that Moses was to ascend Mt. Nebo and see the Promised Land. (See the maps, pages 128 and 146.)

Israelites in the gorge of the Arnon which for brillance of color, compares with the Grand Canyon of the Colorado.

So the Hebrews refused again to fight with kindred races. They left the Plains of Moab and tramped along through the desert till they suddenly came to a halt before the yawning depths of a wild and beautiful gorge, rocky and many-hued, that dropped off abruptly before them. A half a mile below, the roaring torrent of the river Ar'non went tumbling over boulders.

Down the steep, dizzy heights Moses and Joshua led their motley throng of followers—men, women and children, flocks and herds, with camp equipment and luggage. Down cliffs that were almost sheer they climbed, then across the torrent and up the opposite wall.

Thus they came at last to A-ro'er on the northern bank of the Arnon. And Si'hon, an Amorite king, had conquered this country from Moab, and dwelt in the city of Hesh'bon.

And the Israelites sent to Sihon, as they had to the King of Edom, begging permission to pass through his land, paying for food and water. But water was scarce in Heshbon; it had to be fought and toiled for in all the surrounding plain. The people had carefully terraced their hills, making cisterns to catch the rain-water, and the center of life at Heshbon was a wide and beautiful pool, as clear as the eyes of a maiden. Sihon had no mind to share his precious water with strangers who came crowding in such alarming numbers. He went out to fight against them. And Sihon was no kin of Israel; so Israel made no more delay; they smote him with the sword; they slew his sons and his people; they took his land and his cities; they dwelt in Heshbon and all her villages.

Then they skirted the borders of Ammon, and went up northward to Ba'shan, where Og, the giant, was king.

And Og was a man so tall, that, behold, his bedstead was a bedstead of iron, 20 feet long and 6 feet wide. And Og

The giant Og, asleep in his bedstead of iron. Bashan, renowned for its bulls and rams, its pastures, and huge oak trees, lay at the foot of Mt. Hermon, the beautiful snow-capped mountain which dominates all of Palestine. Bedstead copied from a metal bed found at Beth-palet. For a picture of the capital of the Ammonites, see page 415.

A Semitic warrior from an Egyptian tomb painting at El-A-mar'na, showing the short leather skirt and the characteristic weapons, a spear and a short curved knife. Joshua must have worn such a garment and been armed like this. (See page 116.)

came out and all his people to do battle with the Children of Israel. But the Children of Israel slew him and took away all his cities. And his bedstead fell to the Children of Ammon, who kept it in their chief city.

Thus the Children of Israel took all the land east of Jordan, from the the rocky gorge of the Arnon to the glistening snows of Mount Hermon, saving for the land of Ammon. And they pitched their tents by Jordan across from Jericho.

Then Ba'lak, King of Moab, was sore afraid for their multitude and he sent to fetch Ba'laam, the soothsayer, out of the mountains of the East, that he might curse all Israel. But Balaam came to the high places and blessed Israel instead, crying: "Surely the Lord hath blessed thee!"

Now Moses was an old man, and he named Joshua to follow him as leader of the people. Then he went up Mt. Nebo and beheld all the land to the sea, with Jericho, the city of palm trees, lying in the plain below. And the Lord said unto Moses, "This is the land that I promised unto Abraham, Isaac and Jacob. Thou hast seen it with thine eyes; but thou shalt not go over thither."

A scarab (1400-1000 B.C.) discovered at Gezer and showing costumes of the period in Canaan, long Babylonian garments at the left, mingled with Egyptian kilts at the right.

So Moses, the servant of the Lord, died; and the Children of Israel wept for the loss of their first great leader who had brought them out of bondage, given them rules of conduct, made them into a nation, and taught them to know one God.

Joshua, the Warrior

Now Joshua, the son of Nun, was full of the spirit of wisdom, and the Lord spake unto Joshua saying, "As I was with Moses, so I will be with thee. I will not fail thee, nor forsake thee. Be strong and of a good courage; for the Lord thy God is with thee."

And Joshua had it in mind to cross the river Jordan and possess the other side. So he sent two men in secret to make report of the land. And they plunged through a jungle growth of tropical plants and flowers where lions had their lairs, till they stood by the banks of the stream, steaming in blazing sunshine with heat like the heat of a hot-house.

They forded the river and came to a plain, fertile, rich and green, and famous for its palm-trees. And in the midst of that plain, rose the clay-brick walls of Jericho.

And the spies entered in at the gates and found a city, small in extent, with little flat-topped houses huddled on narrow lanes and even bulging over atop the twelve foot wall. And they lodged with a woman named Ra'hab whose house was built on the wall. And it was told the King of Jericho: "Behold there came hither tonight spies of the Children of Israel."

The ruins of Jericho as they are today. Jericho stood in the midst of the verdant plain of palm trees known as the Plain of Jericho This plain, made green in ancient days by the waters of Elijah's fountain, runs between the mountains and the weird lifeless shores of the desolate Dead Sea. Once a crowded mass of houses rose from these stone foundations and overflowed on the wall. Each little square depression in the picture was a whole house. Houses in the old Canaanite towns were so tiny and huddled together, that all of Jericho could be enclosed within a good sized football stadium of today. It was perhaps on this very wall that Rahab's house stood and over this very wall that she let down the spies from her window.

And the King sent to Rahab saying, "Deliver up these men which are entered into thine house."

But Rahab answered, "I cannot; for they left the city at dark, at the time of closing the gate."

And she brought the men up to the roof and hid them mid stalks of flax till the search for them was past. And she said unto them: "I know that the Lord hath given you this land. And now I pray you, since I have showed you kindness, save me and my kindred alive in the day when you take the city."

So they promised to save her alive; and she let them down by a cord through the window and over the wall, that they came outside the city. And they came and said unto Joshua: "Truly the Lord hath delivered the whole land into our hands; for all the inhabitants fear us."

Then Joshua gave command to cross the river Jordan.

The river Jordan near Jericho where the children of Israel crossed. The Jordan, Palestine's only important river is well named the "Down Comer," for, as it twists and turns, it rushes continuously downward till it reaches the salt Dead Sea 1300 feet below the level of the ocean. Its waters were never navigable for ships, and its valley, often shut in by cliffs, was the wilderness of Bible times. Background sketched from a photograph.

Joshua's men attacking the hill town of Ai. Ai stood on a very rocky height, approached from the direction of the Jordan, by a path that even today is remarkably steep and difficult. The stones of Ai are typical of the stones, stones and more stones that abound everywhere in Palestine. Situation sketched from a photograph.

And the Children of Israel crossed with priests at the head of their column bearing the Ark of the Covenant wrapped from sight in its veil.

And they went and laid siege to Jericho; and the city was straightly shut up so that none went out and none came in. And the Children of Israel marched about the walls, preceded by priests who bore the Ark and blew upon ram's horn trumpets. And they took the city and burned it with fire, but Rahab they saved alive.

Then the Children of Israel toiled from the steaming hot plain up a steep and rocky path to the cool hill-town of A'i.

And Joshua chose 5,000 mighty men and sent them away by night to lie in ambush behind the city. And he

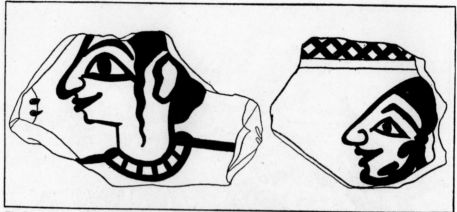

The Canaanites as they saw themselves in Joshua's day. Portraits of a Canaanite man and woman painted on the fragments of a pot found at Beisan, the Bethshan of the Bible.

and all his people of war showed themselves in the valley.

And when the King of Ai saw Joshua and his men, he went out against them to battle; but he wist not that liers-in-ambush were hidden behind the city. And Joshua and all Israel made as if they were beaten before the men of Ai and they fled by way of the wilderness. And all the men of Ai pursued after Joshua and were drawn away from the city.

Then Joshua stretched out his spear and the ambush arose quickly and ran and entered the city and set it afire. And when the men of Ai looked back, behold, the smoke of the city ascended up to heaven and they could not flee this way or that. And Joshua and all Israel turned and slew the men of Ai. And they took the King of Ai and hanged him to a tree.

And when the inhabitants of Gib'e-on, a second hill-town close by, heard what Joshua had done unto Jericho and Ai, they went unto Joshua wilily, as though they were ambassadors come from a city too far away for him to have need to conquer it. And they took old sacks upon their asses, and put old garments upon them and old shoes upon their feet. And they said unto Joshua: "We be come from a far country. Our shoes and our garments were new when we set out from our homes. Make ye a league with us."

And Joshua believed their tale and promised to let them live. But when he learned their deceit and how they dwelt so near, he made them hewers of wood and drawers of water for the camp.

Now in times past, the Pharaoh, Thut'mose III, had taken Canaan for Egypt; but in the days of Akh-na'ton when the Governor of Jerusalem begged in vain for the help of Egyptian arms, the Hittite had made himself master, and the old king Shub'-bi-lu'li-u'ma, dwelling up north in Car'che-mish in his grim and heavy palace, had ruled a great Hittite Empire and been overlord of Canaan. In turn the Hittite had yielded to Ramses II of Egypt, and when the power of Egypt fell, Canaan had broken up into numberless petty kingdoms with kings of towns and villages who ruled a handful of men.

But all these petty kings, Amorites, Canaanites, Hittites, made a league against Joshua. And they camped beside Lake Me'rom as the sand on the sea-shore in multitude. And Joshua came and smote that host and chased them unto Zidon.

A Hittite chariot, riding down a Semite, such as Joshua's followers were. From a Hittite carving found in the public square of the ancient Hittite city of Carchemish. Usually the Hittites rode three powerful warriors in a chariot, a fact which so impressed the Egyptians that when they drew pictures of Hittite chariots, they crowded in a third man, half falling out of the vehicle, in their eagerness to show this strange and remarkable custom. (See Vol. I, p. 231.)

It was an old Hittite king, who used an Amorite prince for his dupe and seized possession of many cities in Canaan in the days when the Pharaoh Akhnaton, was overlord of the land. A clay letter is still in existence, found at El-Amarna in Egypt, and written by the Egyptian governor of Jerusalem, begging Akhnaton for help, and piteously pleading that he can hold out no longer—but must soon surrender to the foe. (See V. I, 216.) In these days Babylonian, Egyptian and Hittite influences were everywhere strong in the arts and industries of Canaan.

Canaanite warriors of Joshua's time as their own people saw them. Figures of about 1300 B. C. painted on a vase found at Me-gid'do. The sole garment of these warriors is a short, triangular bright-colored piece of breast-armor, probably of wood, with brown black bosses of metal. In the left hand they carry a small round shield; in the right hand a hatchet or battle axe. See the figures of the naked giants, page 133.

Doubtless many common soldiers were thus scantily clothed though the Pharaoh Thutmose III who once took the city of Megiddo, listed among the spoils taken, a beautiful bronze shirt of mail, of the prince of Megiddo, and two hundred shirts of mail of his "wretched soldiers."

And Joshua cut off the An'a-kims, the giants, till there were none left in the land save only in Ga'za, in Gath, and

Map of Canaan as divided among the Twelve Tribes.

in Ash'dod, cities of the Philis-tines. And Joshua smote one and thirty kings on the west side of the Jordan, and he took the whole land, from the southward near Mount Se'ir to the valley of the Leb'a-non.

Then he set up the taber-nacle at Shi'loh, and he divid-ed the land by lot among the twelve tribes of Israel, three tribes east of Jordan, nine tribes west, and the tribe of Levi to serve the tabernacle, having no land allotted to them, but dwelling in forty-eight cities.

Joshua's men encountering Hittites, Amorites, and Canaanites before the Canaanite stronghold of Hazor. In the background to the left towers Mt. Hermon, to the right gleam the waters of Lake Merom. Hazor is reconstructed after descriptions of the discoveries made there by Professor J. Garstang, Director of Antiquities in Palestine. Professor Garstang says that Hazor was a fortified camp large enough to contain a permanent garrison of 40,000 or 50,000 men. It stood at the junction of the main roads into Palestine from Sidon and Damascus.

The road to Sidon is the one swinging off northward to the left at the top of the picture. This same road, wandering off southward in the foreground leads to Megiddo and Bethsan. The road crossing the picture horizontally, leads on the right, east and northward to Damascus.

The walls of Hazor rose in the front to a height of 185 feet above the water course at its feet. In the rear, it was also shut in by a water course and to the south east by a rain-scoured gully. In the foreground of the fortress is a raised platform paved with stone and containing permanent stone buildings. In the rear is a second stone edifice. Between are the tents and frail wooden structures of the camp. Joshua XI: 10-13 tells how Joshua took and destroyed this fortress.

Thanks to the work of Joshua, the Children of Israel entered in and possessed the Promised Land. But Joshua said: "Take good heed to yourselves; for if ye make marriages with the nations round about and serve their gods, the Lord will no more drive them out before you; but they shall be snares and traps to you, till ye perish from off this land."

The Judges of Israel

Now Israel served the Lord all the days of Joshua and all the days of the elders which overlived Joshua. But there arose another generation which knew not the Lord, nor yet the works which he had done for Israel; and they left off wandering and living in tents and began to build them houses and settle down in cities; and they took the daughters of the Canaanites, and of the Amorites, and of the Hittites to be their wives, and they copied the Canaanite customs, serving the Ba'als on the high places beneath the sacred poles.

And these nations round about thought of their gods as like themselves, changeful, tyrannical, cruel, delighting in drunken mirth and bloody sacrifice. Such gods never made their people over after any pattern of goodness and perfection, for they shared every human fault. Only the God of the Hebrews, whose nature was slowly being discerned by the clearest Hebrew thinkers, had an absolute standard of right and wrong apart from human judgments, a standard to make life better and happier for men.

A sacrifice on a Canaanite high place as the Canaanites of this age saw it.

A very finely carved seal from Gezer (1400-1000 B.C.), showing four figures in embroidered robes, carrying a knife and scimitar and about to offer sacrifice with animal heads and a vase.

The customs of the people round about, cruel and bestial, did indeed tempt the Hebrews away from their budding vision of God.

The wholesale slaughter of Joshua in wiping out Israel's foes often seems needlessly cruel, until one sees that without it, these nations would have absorbed Israel, foisted their views upon her, and snuffed out that religion which was to grow and unfold till it blossomed in Christianity.

At each stage of their progress, the wise-men of Israel did what was necessary in that age to preserve as much of the knowledge of God as they had been able to attain.

Thus their religion lived and advanced by progressive steps, while the beautiful vision of Akhnaton which he sought to put into effect all at once, vanished from the earth. See Vol. I, p. 220.

Serving the gods of the high-places brutalized mankind, and the people whom the Hebrews left in the Land of Canaan, became, as Joshua had foretold, a snare and a trap unto them, confusing their budding vision and tempting them back to evil. Lower and lower they sank, their vision of God's protecting power darkened and almost lost.

Two men on either side of a sacred tree with two stags beside them. From a seal discovered at Gezer. The sacred tree appears often in these seals. It was the symbol of the worship of the female goddess of fertility Ashtoreth, Astarte, or Ishtar, the companion of the male God Baal; and because it stood only for material growth, it was the center of a religion with all sorts of bestial rites and wild and wanton festivities.

Now they served the Moabites, now the Canaanites, now the Ammonites, till judges rose up to free them, rude, half-barbarous chieftains, living in barbarous days, but sometimes catching glimpses again of the power of the living God.

Fifteen of these judges arose at different times in the land, for there was no king in Israel. The tribes had no central government; they looked on God as their king and were loosely joined together in a sort of federation.

Among these judges was Gid'e-on, the farmer lad, who left the threshing of wheat to drive out hosts of Arabs, taking only 300 men with neither swords nor weapons and rushing at night on the Arab host, blowing trumpets and brandishing lamps till the foe in wild confusion, fell on each other and fled.

A second carving of a man with a sacred tree from a seal found at Gezer. The parade of birds is interesting. More interesting material has been excavated at Gezer than at any other Bible City, and the "Excavation of Gezer" by Robert MacAlister is a mine of information for students. Gezer is mentioned in the Bible, in Joshua 10:33, 12:12, 16:10 and in many other places.

And Gideon the people would have made their king, but he said unto them: "I will not rule over you, neither shall my son rule over you. The Lord shall be your king."

Cretan men and women, the women copied from Cretan carvings and paintings, the men from Egyptian paintings. These interesting and highly civilized people, when driven by Greek barbarians from their island of Crete, became the sea-rovers, called on Egyptian monuments Pulosathu or Philistines which meant "immigrants."
The Philistines settled in Palestine just before the Hebrews, and from them Palestine was named. See Volume III, Chapter I.

And when the Children of Israel had subdued the people of Canaan, the Canaanites, Amorites, Hittites, there still remained a foreign race but newly come to the sea-coast, who fought with exceeding courage for dominion over the land.

The great sea battle wherein Ramses III defeated these sea-rovers, the Philistines, and drove them away from Egypt, making it necessary for them to settle on the coast plains of Canaan. The scene sculptured on the walls of Ramses' temple at Thebes. See Vol. I, pp. 235, 236.
Of the nine ships engaged, the four having lion's heads at the prow are Egyptian. Three are at the left, and one in the lower right hand corner. The other five ships with goose-heads and long goose necks belong to the Philistines. All the Philistines have feathered head-dresses (see the pictures on page 152).
The Egyptians are over-whelming the enemy with volleys of arrows from their bows, but the Philistines have no arrows. They have only round shields and spears or two-edged swords.
Philistine prisoners may be seen bound in the Egyptian boats (recognizable by their feathered head-dresses), while one Philistine boat in the middle of the bottom row has over-turned and thrown its crew in the ocean.

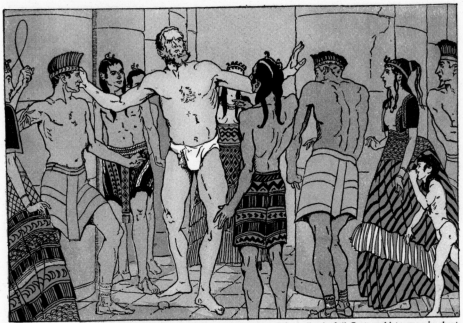

Samson in the temple, mocked by the Philistine lords and ladies; ladies in full Cretan skirts, men in short Cretan waistcloth; soldiers in feathered head-dress. Samson was the thirteenth judge or leader of the Israelites.
Before Samuel came (1) Oth-ni'el, (2) Ehud, who stabbed the fat tyrant of Moab as he sat in his summer-parlor, (3) Shamgar, who slew the Philistines with an ox-goad; (4) Barak and Deborah, the woman, (5) Gideon, (6) A-bim'e-lech, (7) To'la, (8) Jair, (9) the wild outlaw chieftain Jephthah, (10) Ib'zan, (11) E'lon, (12) Abdon, and (13) Samson. After Samson came Eli, the high priest at Shiloh, and Samuel, the last great judge.

These people were the Philistines, children of the old sea-kings, from the distant island of Crete; they who built the palace at Knos'sus, the houses with elaborate bathrooms, and the stadium for bull-grappling, where boy and girl toreadors caught the bull by the horns and vaulted over his back. They had been driven from Crete by hordes of wild Greek warriors, and joining with other sea rovers had come in their swift war galleys bearing down upon Egypt in the days of Ramses III.

But Ramses defeated the Philistines and threw them back from Egypt, and so they had crossed the sea to the rich coast-plains of Canaan, where their people already had trading posts; and there, just before the Hebrews arrived, they

The Philistines with feathered head-dresses, as the Assyrians saw them.   From Layard's Monuments of Nineveh.

settled in five confederate towns, Gath, Ga'za, Ash'ke-lon, Ash'dod and Ek'ron, each governed by a king.   Their warriors wore bronze armor and round head dresses of feathers; they knew how to work in metal, how to make

The Philistines with their feathered head-dresses as the Egyptians saw them.   A carving from the temple of Ramses III at Thebes.   Note their stiff leather skirts.

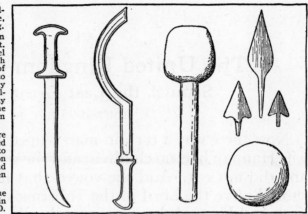

Weapons found in tombs in Palestine; a dagger, a scimitar, a mace, arrows, and a large ball for a sling.

The presence of iron knives in some of these tombs is of interest. A passage in the Bible, (I Samuel 13:19) says that there was no smith found throughout all the land of Israel, and that the Israelites had to seek to the Philistines whenever they needed a smith. Moreover, the Philistines kept swords and spears away from the Israelites so that in all the land of Israel, only Saul and his son Jonathan owned swords.

Evidently the Philistines were already in the iron age, but allowed only an occasional weapon to get into Israel. Doubtless that is one reason why Shamgar used an ox-goad and Samson the jaw-bone of an ass, when they attacked the Philistines.

Unquestionably in this age, the Philistines far excelled the Hebrews in art and general culture. See page 170.

swords and spears; and the Hebrews had to seek unto them whenever they needed a blacksmith. They far excelled the Hebrews in culture and every art, and gained a dominion over them, which none among the judges could ever entirely break.

Samson, the strong man of Israel, helped his people against them. He tore down the gates of Gaza and bore them away on his back. But Samson was betrayed to the lords of the Philistines by De-li′lah, the woman he loved. His eyes were put out and he was cast into prison in Gaza, and set to grinding corn. And when the lords of the Philistines made merry and gathered together for to offer sacrifices unto Da′gon, their god, they fetched Samson from the prison-house to make them sport. And ladies in full Cretan skirts, and men in gay Cretan waistcloths, looked down and laughed at blind Samson, as their fathers had laughed at the toreadors vaulting over the bulls. And Samson took hold of two pillars of the temple and pulled the whole building down on himself and all the people therein. But the Children of Israel still remained subject unto Philistia.

VI

The United Kingdom of Israel

Samuel, the Last Great Judge

(About 1095 b. c.)

Now there was a certain man named El-ka'nah, and his wife Hannah had no children; and she was grieved and wept and did not eat. And she vowed that if she had a son, he should serve the Lord in the Tabernacle all the days of his life. And Hannah bare a son and called his name Samuel. And when she had weaned him, she took three bullocks, an ephah of flour and a bottle of wine, and brought him unto the House of the Lord in Shiloh, unto E'li, the High Priest.

And the child did minister unto the Lord; and his mother made him a little coat, and brought it to him from year to year when she came up with her husband to offer the yearly sacrifice. And Samuel grew and the Lord was with him.

And Samuel judged Israel; but the Philistines came and took the Ark of God in battle; and they kept it for seven months till they were troubled with plagues. Then they said: "It is because we have stolen the Ark." And they put the Ark on a cart and turned the kine loose; and the kine took the straight road to Beth-she'mesh. And Israelites were reaping their wheat in the valley and they lifted up their eyes and saw the Ark and rejoiced to see it return.

And Samuel said: "Put away strange gods and serve God only and God will deliver you from the Philistines."

And Israel obeyed, and the Philistines came no more against Israel all the days of Samuel.

But it came to pass when Samuel was old, that he made his sons judges over Israel. And his sons took bribes and perverted judgment. Then all the Elders of Israel said

The kine bear the Ark of the Covenant unguided, from Philistia to Israel's frontier-town, Beth'she'mesh.

unto Samuel, "Thy sons walk not in thy ways. Therefore make us a king to judge us like all the other nations."

But the thing displeased Samuel and he said: "If ye ask a king, ye reject the rule of the Lord your God. A king will take your sons for his chariots, and to reap his harvests. He will take your daughters to be confectionaries and cooks. He will take the tenth of your produce. Say not: 'A king shall reign over us'; for the Lord your God is your king."

Nevertheless, the people said: "Give us a king."

Saul, the First King
(About 1095-1055 b. c.)

Now there was a man of the tribe of Benjamin whose name was Kish, and he had a son named Saul, a choice young man and a goodly. From his shoulders and upwards he was higher than any of the people. And the asses of Kish were lost, and Saul and a servant went out to seek them; but they found them not. And when they came unto Ramah, Saul said: "Let us return, lest my father be anxious about us."

But the servant said: "Behold, in yonder city is a man of God. Peradventure he can tell us where to find the asses."

And when they were come to the gate of the city, they met Samuel going up to the high place for to offer the sacrifice.

And Samuel said unto Saul: "Go up before me; for thou shalt be king in Israel."

And Saul was astonished and said: "My family is small in importance. Wherefore should I be king?"

But Samuel took Saul and his servant into the guest-chamber, and made them sit in the chiefest place. And thereafter he talked with Saul on the housetop. And the next day he rose up early and walked with Saul to the gate of the city. Then he sent Saul's servant on before, and he took a vial of oil and anointed Saul's head in secret. And he said: "The Lord hath anointed thee king over Israel."

So Saul departed and found the asses; but of the matter of the kingdom, he spake to no one. And Samuel called the people to Miz'pah to choose a king by lot. And Saul was chosen; but when they sought him he could not be found, for he had hid himself amid the circle of baggage that surrounded the encampment. And they ran and fetched him thence, and he stood higher than all the people.

And Samuel said: "Behold whom the Lord hath chosen!"

And all the people shouted: "God save the king!"

But when Saul was gone home to Gib'e-ah, certain men despised him, saying: "How shall this fellow save us?"

Then came Na'hash, the Ammonite, and laid siege to a town of Israel. And the townsmen were sore pressed and cried: "Make peace with us! We will serve thee!"

But Nahash answered fiercely: "On this condition will I make peace,—that ye let me thrust out your right eyes!"

And messengers brought the tidings to Gibeah, and all the people lifted up their voices and wept. And, behold, Saul came from his work following the cattle out of the field, and a fiery rage came upon him when he heard the words of Nahash; and he slew a yoke of oxen and sent the pieces thereof throughout all Israel, saying: "Whosoever cometh not forth after Saul and after Samuel to deliver his land from the Ammonite, so shall it be done to his oxen!"

A seal of the period discovered at Gezer. The standing figure in the long robe might well be Samuel, the seated figure Saul, the third man an attendant, and beside him, Saul's spear stuck in the ground.

And the people came with one consent, and gathered themselves unto Saul. And they slew the Ammonites until the heat of the day. And when the people saw Saul victorious, they said unto Samuel: "Who questioned Saul's right to rule us? Let such men be put to death."

But Saul said: "There shall not a man be put to death today; for today the Lord hath wrought salvation in Israel."

And all the people went to Gil'gal and made Saul king.

And in the second year of his reign, the Philistines gathered themselves together to fight with Israel, 30,000 chariots, 6,000 horsemen, and people as the sands on the sea-shore. And the men of Israel fled before them and hid themselves in caves, and in thickets, and in rocks, and in high places, and in pits. And they gathered themselves together, trembling, unto Saul at Gilgal.

And Saul tarried seven days, waiting for Samuel to come and offer sacrifice, as was the right of the priest. But Samuel came not; and Saul was impatient of soul and recklessly went himself and offered the sacrifice. Then Samuel came and said: "Thou hast done foolishly. Thou hast rashly exalted thyself. Thy kingdom shall not continue."

And Saul did evil again; and Samuel came no more to see Saul until the day of his death. But he went unto Jesse, the Beth'le-hem-ite, of the tribe of Judah, to anoint another king. And Jesse made seven of his sons to pass before Samuel, and Samuel looked on the eldest, a tall and stately lad, and he said: "Surely the Lord's anointed is before him."

But the Lord said unto Samuel, "Look not on his countenance nor on the height of his stature, for the Lord seeth not as man seeth, for man looketh on the outward appearance, but the Lord looketh on the heart."

And Samuel said unto Jesse: "Are here all thy children?"

And Jesse said: "Behold, the youngest keepeth the sheep." And he sent and fetched David, a ruddy lad, fair of eyes. And the Lord said unto Samuel: "Anoint him, for this is he."

Then Samuel took a horn of oil and anointed David in the midst of his brethren. And David returned to his flocks; and the spirit of the Lord came upon him from that day forward. And to him, the heavens at night-time declared the glory of God with the brilliance of moon and stars. He looked on the light of the morning when the sky is without a cloud; he saw the tender grass springing up out of the earth by clear shining after rain; and the whole world seemed to him to skip, to sing, to shout, for joy of God, its creator. And his soul was filled with praise for the glory and beauty of God, and the glory and beauty of man whom God had crowned with honor. And he sang with reverent love:

> "The pastures are clothed with flocks;
> The valleys also are covered over with corn;
> They shout for joy, they also sing!
> Make a joyful noise unto God; all ye lands,
> All the earth shall worship thee and shall sing unto thee;
> They shall sing to thy name."

And there came a lion and took a lamb out of his flock. And David said in his heart: "It is God that girdeth me with strength," and he caught the lion by his beard and slew him and delivered the lamb. And God seemed to David like a good shepherd ever guarding his people as a shepherd guardeth his flocks; and he sang in confident trust:

"The Lord is my shepherd, I shall not want;
He maketh me to lie down in green pastures,
He leadeth me beside the still waters;
He restoreth my soul.

Yea, though I walk through the Valley of the Shadow of Death,
I will fear no evil; for Thou art with me;
Thy rod and Thy staff they comfort me.
Thou preparest a table before me in the presence of mine enemies;
Thou anointest my head with oil; my cup runneth over;

Surely goodness and mercy shall follow me all the days of my life,
And I will dwell in the house of the Lord forever."

But the spirit of the Lord departed from Saul and he was troubled with madness. And Saul's servants said unto him: "Command us to seek out a cunning player upon an harp, for when the frenzy is on thee, he shall play and thou wilt be well."

And Saul heard say that David, son of Jesse, played well; and he sent unto Jesse and said: "Send me David, thy son."

And Jesse laded an ass with bread, and a bottle of wine, and a kid, and sent them by David unto Saul. And when the frenzy was upon Saul, David played before him, fresh and innocent music, full of his trust in God and joy in His creation. So Saul was refreshed and was well and the madness departed from him. And Saul loved David greatly and made him his armor-bearer.

Now the Philistines gathered together their armies to battle; and they stood on a mountain on the one side, and Israel stood on a mountain on the other side, and there was a valley between them.

And there went out a champion of the camp of the Philistines named Go-li'ath of Gath, whose height was six cubits and a span. And he had an helmet of brass on his head and greaves of brass on his legs and he was armed with a coat of mail. And one bearing a shield went before him.

And Goliath cried to the armies of Israel morning and evening for forty days, saying: "Choose ye a man that he may come down unto me! If he kill me, then will we be your servants, but if I kill him, then shall ye be our servants! I defy the armies of Israel this day!"

And Saul and his host were greatly afraid.

Now the three eldest sons of Jesse followed Saul to the battle; therefore David went home to keep his father's sheep. But Jesse said unto David: "Take thou an ephah of corn and ten loaves and run to the camp to look how thy brethren fare. And carry these ten cheeses to the captain of their thousand."

So David left his sheep in the care of a keeper and went. And he came to the place of wagons as the host was going forth, shouting to the battle. And David left his baggage with the keeper of the baggage and ran into the army that he might salute his brethren.

And behold there came up the champion, Goliath of Gath; and all the men of Israel fled and were sore afraid.

And David said: "Who is this Philistine that he should defy the armies of the living God?"

Then E-li'ab, David's brother, cried: "Why camest thou hither, and with whom hast thou left thy sheep? I know thy pride and the naughtiness of thine heart! Thou art come to see the battle."

But David said unto Saul: "Let no man's heart fail because of this Philistine. Thy servant will go and fight him."

And Saul said to David: "Thou art not able to go; for thou art only a youth, and this giant a man of war."

But David said: "The Lord that delivered me out of the paws of the lion, and out of the paws of a bear, He will deliver me from this Philistine."

Then Saul said unto David: "Go and the Lord be with thee."

And he armed David with his coat of mail and with his sword; but David said unto Saul: "I cannot go with these, for I have not proved them."

And he took them off, and put the sword away, and chose

A fine Hebrew carving of a lion, cut on a rectangular disc and found at Gezer. The figure, done in the period of David, indicates how common lions were in Palestine in that day.

David and Goliath of Gath fight in the Valley of Elah (Background from a photograph) Israelites encamped on the hill to the left and Philistines to the right. Goliath's feathered head-dress is from paintings, page 152. Goliath was of the ancient race of huge men, the An'a-kim, whom Joshua found in Canaan and whom he destroyed entirely except for a few who settled in Gath and other Philistine cities (Joshua 11:22). See pages 133, 139, 146.

him five smooth stones out of the brook. And he put the stones in his shepherd's bag. And his sling was in his hand.

And the Philistine drew near and the man that bare the shield went before him. And Goliath disdained David, because he was but a youth, ruddy and fair of face, and he cursed David by his gods and cried: "Come to me and I will give thy flesh unto the fowls of the air and to the beasts of the field!"

Then said David to the Philistine: "Thou comest to me with a sword and with a spear and with a shield, but I come to thee in the name of the Lord of Hosts, the God of the armies of Israel whom thou hast defied. This day will the Lord deliver thee into mine hand. And all this assembly shall know that the Lord saveth not with sword and spear, for the battle is the Lord's."

And David ran to meet the Philistine. And he put his hand in his bag and took thence a stone and slang it and smote the Philistine in the forehead. And behold, the Philistine fell flat on his face to the earth. And David ran and drew the Philistine's sword and cut off his head. And when the Philistines saw that their champion was dead, they arose and fled; and Israel pursued them.

Now Saul's son, Jonathan, loved David as his own soul, and he made a covenant with him. And Jonathan stripped himself of his robes, and of his bow and of his girdle and even of his sword, and he gave them to David. And Saul set David over his men of war and all Israel and Judah loved David. But it came to pass when David returned

Saul, in his jealousy, casting a javelin to smite David. The frieze of birds on the wall is copied from a design discovered at Gezer; the tripod with a woman blowing a flute, decorating the standard, was discovered at Megiddo, and shows the crudeness of actual Hebrew work of the period. The pots are copied from pots of the period found at Gezer and show the designs of birds and quaint animals replacing earlier geometric designs.

Michal lets David down through a window.   The fate of Michal after this was sad.   During David's long years of enforced outlawry, Saul gave Michal to another husband, and it was not until after Saul's death, that David forced this second husband to return Michal.   By that time her heart seems to have changed toward David, for in the day of his greatest triumph when he brought the ark up to Jerusalem, it is written that she "despised him in her heart," and mocked at him because he had put his royal dignity aside and danced before the ark.   And David put her away thereafter, and she was no longer his wife.   See page 172.

from battle, that the women came out of all the cities of
Israel, singing and dancing to meet King Saul with tabors,
with joy, and with instruments of music. And they said:

> "Saul has slain his thousands,
> And David his tens of thousands."

And Saul was very wroth and he said: "They have ascribed
unto David ten thousands and to me they have ascribed but
thousands, and what can he have more but the kingdom."

And Saul eyed David with jealousy from that day forward, and when the madness came upon him, he cast a
javelin to smite David; but Jonathan pleaded for David,
and Mi'chal, Saul's daughter, loved him; and Saul hearkened unto Jonathan and he gave Michal to David to wife.

Nevertheless, when David went again against the Philistines, Saul's jealousy returned and he cast his javelin once
more. And David fled to his home. And Saul sent mes-

sengers unto David's house to lie in wait and slay him in the morning. And Michal said unto David: "Save thyself tonight, or tomorrow thou shalt be slain."

And Michal let David down through a window and he fled. And Michal took an image and laid it in David's bed and she put a pillow of goat's hair for his bolster and covered it with cloth. And when Saul's messengers came, they found only the image in the bed.

Then Saul was wroth with Jonathan because of his friendship with David, and he cast a javelin at Jonathan, crying: "Thou son of a perverse, rebellious woman, thou hast chosen the son of Jesse to thy confusion; for as long as he liveth thou shalt not be king after me."

But Jonathan loved David and thought not of himself.

And David returned no more to court, but dwelt in the cave A-dul'lam, and everyone that was in distress, or discontented, or in debt, gathered themselves unto him, about four hundred in number, and he became captain over them.

And David and his men saved the town of Ke-i'lah from the Philistines who robbed the threshing floors. But the men of Keilah told Saul that David was within their gates,

The goats who were David's companions on the crags, and a wild bird or two, as the Hebrews of the period painted them on their pottery. See the vase page 164. David is repeatedly said to have fled to the crags of the wild goats.

David and his men lead the wild lives of outlaws. Background of this picture copied from a photograph of the wilderness of En-ge'di, showing the Dead Sea in the distance.

and David and his men fled and hid themselves in the wood, in a mountain in the wilderness of Ziph. And Saul sought him every day. But Jonathan went to David to comfort him in the wood. And he said: "Fear not! Thou shalt be king over Israel, and I will be second to thee."

Then the men of Ziph would have delivered David unto Saul; but David went up from thence and dwelt in the wilderness of En-ge'di. And Saul took three thousand chosen men and went to seek David upon the crags of the wild goats. And many a time in those days the heart of David was sore and he cried: "They that hate me without a cause are more than the hairs of mine head! My God, my God, why hast thou forsaken me!"

David's companions, the wild stags of the mountain, as the Hebrews saw them. Beautifully carved stags and the favorite guilloche pattern of twisted strands, carved on a seal discovered at Gezer.

But his soul thirsted after God, to see His power and His glory so as he had seen it in the clear, calm days of his youth. And his confidence returned and he sang:

"The Lord is my light and my salvation;
    Whom shall I fear?
The Lord is the strength of my life;
    Of whom shall I be afraid?
Though an host should encamp against me,
    My heart shall not fear."

And Saul came to the sheepfolds where was a cave and he went in and lay down. And David and his men were hiding in the innermost parts of the cave. And the men said unto David: "Behold, thine enemy is in thine hands. Do to him as seemest good unto thee."

Then David arose and cut off the skirt of Saul's robe. But his heart smote him for what he had done; and he suffered not his servants to rise against Saul, for he cried when Saul went out of the cave: "My Lord, the King."

And Saul looked behind him, and David stooped with his face to the earth and said: "Wherefore hearest thou

A man in a belt and necklace, such scanty clothing as David's men must often have worn. The man is pulling up a bush by the roots, as David's men may sometimes have done when greatly in need of food. Beside him sit two stags, suitable comrades for outlaws.

men's words, saying, 'David seekest my hurt'? Look, my father, see! The skirt of thy robe is in my hand. I cut off thy skirt, but killed thee not; and yet thou huntest my life.''

And Saul said: "Is this thy voice, my son David? Thou art more righteous than I, for thou hast rewarded me good for evil.'' And he lifted up his voice and wept.

Nevertheless, David and his men gat them up again to their strongholds; and they lived the lives of outlaws, in caves and forests or on high mountain-crags, companions only to shepherds, whom they entreated well, neither stole they aught from the shepherds; for they asked their food of rich husbandmen when they held a sheep-shearing feast, or were gladdened perchance by a gift of bread and raisins and cake, brought them by some good woman, riding upon an ass.

And no sooner was Samuel dead, than Saul came once again, following after David as one doth hunt a partridge.

And David crept into Saul's camp by night and came

where Saul lay sleeping. And he took the spear that stood
in the ground by the side of Saul, and the cruse of water
at his head; but he touched not Saul because he was the
Lord's anointed.

Then David sought refuge of the Philistines in Gath;
and Saul sought no more for him.

But it came to pass in process of time that the Philistines
came again to give battle unto Israel; and when Saul saw
their host, he was sore afraid and did evil again; for he
disguised himself and went to the Witch of En'dor, a
woman that had a familiar spirit, such an one as God had
commanded Saul to put away out of the land. And Saul
bade the Witch of Endor to show him Samuel, which was
dead, that he might enquire of Samuel concerning the fate
of Israel. And he saw as it were, the appearance of Samuel,
foretelling grave disaster. And Saul fell on his face on the
earth and there was no strength left in him.

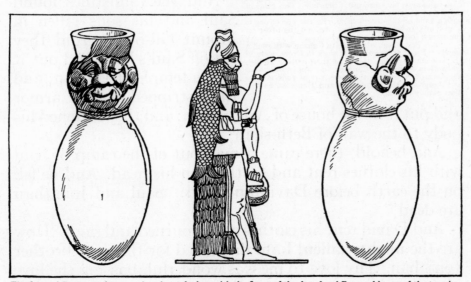

The fish-god Dagon, and two quaint views of a jug, with the figure of the dwarf-god Bes used in one of the temples
of Bethshan, the city where the Philistines took Saul's body and his armor. The jugs were found in Bethshan.

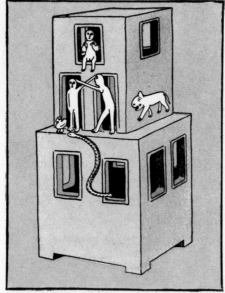

The altar of Ashtoreth, discovered at Bethshan, and doubtless the very one which stood in the temple where Saul's armor was hung. The altar is made of pottery in three stages.

On the uppermost stage is a figure of a seated goddess, who must be Ashtoreth. She holds two birds in her arms. Below on the second stage are two men, each with a hand on the other's head. By the side of one is a bird, and under him a snake. Behind the other on the second stage is the figure of a lioness.

The Philistines, who came to Canaan with such a wonderful past of beautiful art-work in Crete, were in the last stages of the decline of their artistic ability, when they arrived in Canaan, and apparently soon degenerated to making the same sort of rude statues and designs as the Canaanites and Hebrews, as this altar plainly shows.

And the battle went sore against Saul, and the men of Israel fled. And the Philistines followed hard after Saul, and they slew Jonathan and other two sons of Saul. And the archers hit Saul and he was sore wounded. Then said Saul to his armor-bearer: "Draw thy sword and thrust me through."

But his armor-bearer would not. So Saul took a sword and fell upon it. And when his armor-bearer saw that Saul was dead, he fell likewise on the sword and died.

And the Philistines found Saul and his sons fallen in Mount Gil-bo'a. And they cut off Saul's head and put it in the temple of Da'gon; and they stripped off his armor and put it in the house of Ash'to-reth; and they fastened his body to the wall of Beth-shan.

And behold, there came a man out of the camp of Saul with his clothes rent and earth upon his head. And he fell on the earth before David and said: "Saul and Jonathan are dead!"

And David rent his clothes and mourned and said: "How are the mighty fallen! I am distressed for thee, my brother Jonathan. Thy love to me was wonderful, passing the love of women."

The Jebusites taunt David by placing their blind and lame on the wall of their ancient fortress at Jerusalem. It is probable that the Salem whose priest-King Mel-chis'e-dek went out to meet Abraham when he returned from the battle with the Four Kings, about 2100 B.C., was Jerusalem. Jerusalem is first mentioned in historical records in the clay letter written by the Egyptian governor of Jerusalem and begging help of Pharaoh Akhnaton about 1300 B.C. This letter was recently found at El-Amarna in Egypt. See V.I, 216. Mt. Moriah rises beyond the walls.

David, the Great King

(ABOUT 1055-1015 B.C.)

Then David went up to Hebron and the men of Judah made him king over Judah. But Abner, captain of the hosts of Saul, made Ish-bo'sheth, son of Saul, king over Israel; and there was long war between the house of Saul and the house of David.

And Jo'ab, David's friend, fought with Abner at Gibeon, and Abner was beaten and fled. Nevertheless, in his flight, Abner slew Joab's brother, who pursued him, fleet as a roe.

And it came to pass after seven years that Abner quarreled with Ish-bo'sheth and came to join David at Hebron.

And David received Abner kindly, but Joab trusted him not, because he had slain his brother; and when Abner set forth to return again to his home, Joab sent messengers unto the well of Si'rah, to bring him back to Hebron.

And Joab took Abner aside in the gate as if to speak to

him quietly; and he smote him till he died. And when David heard it, he lamented and Joab he sternly rebuked.

But the hands of Saul's son were feeble, as soon as Abner was dead, and two captains of Israel slew him, and all the tribes of Israel anointed David king.

Thereafter, David went up from Hebron to possess himself of Jerusalem, an ancient mountain fastness where dwelt the Jeb'u-sites (for the children of Israel had not yet taken that stronghold).

And the Jebusites mocked at David; for they thought their city so strong that he could never take it. And they set their blind and their lame on the walls to be for a taunt unto David. And they cried aloud to his men: "The blind and the lame are enough to defend these walls. Except thou take them away, thou shalt not come in hither!"

Nevertheless, in the cliff, far below their ancient stronghold, there lay a hidden spring to which they had built a tunnel cut straight down through the rock. And David knew of that spring and that tunnel within the rock whereby they drew up their water. And David cried to his men: "Whosoever goeth up first by way of the gutter and smiteth the Jebusites, he shall be chief and captain over the host!"

And his men went secretly into the cave by the spring, and Joab went up first through the tunnel in the rock; and Joab surprised the city and took it. Therefore Joab became Chief of David's host.

And David dwelt in Jerusalem and repaired it and made it the capital of his kingdom. Therefore they call it the City of David. And David said:" Let us bring the Ark of our God up hither; for we enquired not at it all the days of Saul."

And David and all Israel put the Ark on a new cart drawn by oxen and they brought it up with shouting and with

Valley of Hinnom

Tyropoean Valley

Mt Zion

Mt. Moriah the Temple Hill

Hill of Ophel

Spring

Kedron Valley

DOHN D. CRANE

David's men approach the old Jebusite stronghold of Jerusalem, with the entrance to the spring below. This oldest city of Jerusalem was built on the small pear-shaped Hill of Ophel, and was protected on three sides by the sheer drop of its cliffs to the Kedron and Tyropaean Valleys, the narrow neck of the hill being defended by a moat which separated it from the higher Mt. Moriah, later to be bought by David as the place where he "builded an altar" and where Solomon built the temple; but in these days, as the picture shows, the threshing floor of Ornan, the Jebusite.

The course of the old walls of this very ancient city may be traced today in Jerusalem; the very tunnel through which Joab went up has been discovered, leading straight up through the rock from the Virgin's Spring; and ruins of the large tower at the right may still be seen by visitors as a witness to David's work.

David's wall was built like the old Jebusite wall, of medium sized, rudely rounded, irregular stones, put together with no mortar, the cracks between merely filled up with small stones; but directly next the wall of David's building is some repair work done by Solomon, his son, and the immense difference appears at once,— David's stones are rudely chipped with no chisel, but with a hammer, probably of stone; Solomon's are finely squared and smoothly chiseled blocks, made by the far superior metal tools of his Phoenician workmen and they are fitted squarely together with no cracks between. It is clear that the real civilization of the Hebrews was due to the wisdom of Solomon who introduced foreign skill to Jerusalem.

The background of this picture was made from a sketch based on the results of excavations and reconstructed by *E. F. Beaumont, American Colony, Jerusalem.*

dancing, with sound of the cornet, and with trumpets, and with cymbals, and with harps. And they set the Ark in the middle of the tent that David had pitched for it; and they offered burnt offerings before God. And David made many sweet psalms to sing before the Lord. Therefore did men call him the sweet psalmist of Israel.

And David had many wives and many sons. And he built him a palace in Jerusalem; and Hiram, the Phoeni'cian, King of Tyre, the foremost city of sea-going traders

David walking on the roof-top.   In Palestine, the roofs were flat, surrounded by a little parapet; and people often walked or sat on their roof-tops.   Samuel communed with Saul on his housetop at Rama (see page 156).

in all the ancient world, sent him sweet smelling cedars from Lebanon with masons and carpenters to build the house.

And it was in David's mind likewise to build an house for the Ark, a temple to the Lord; but because he had been a man of war, the Lord forbade him, saying: "Thy son shall be a man of rest.   He shall build Me an house."

So David set himself to gather gold and silver, brass, and iron, and stone, that his son might make the house of fame and glory throughout all lands.   And David subdued the Philistines, the Moabites, the Syrians, and the Edomites, and they sent and paid him tribute.

And David likewise subdued the children of Ammon, but while his men besieged Rabbath, the capital city of Ammon, David tarried at Jerusalem.   And at eventide he arose from his bed and walked on the roof of the palace.   And from the roof he saw a woman bathing.   And the woman was very beautiful; and David sent and enquired after her.   And it was told him she was Bath-she'ba, the wife of U-ri'ah, the Hittite, a good and valiant man, then with the army at Rabbath Ammon.

And David was sore tempted and he wrote a letter unto Joab, the captain of the host, saying: "Set ye Uriah in the forefront of the battle and retire ye from him that he die."

And Joab assigned Uriah unto a place for valiant men. And the men of the city came out and fought in the field, and Joab's men went after them even to the gates of the city; and the shooters shot from the walls and many fell, and Uriah, the Hittite, died.

Then David took Bathsheba, when her days of mourning were over, and made her his wife and she bare him a son. But the thing was a grievous sin and the child of Bathsheba died, and David cried to the Lord in passionate repentance:

Joab assigns Uriah to the forefront of the battle at Rabbath Ammon. Background sketched from photographs taken by the editor. The capital of the turbulent Ammonites was four days journey by caravan east of Jerusalem. It stood on a rocky hill at the head of a spring and the chief feature of the landscape was a beautiful brook flowing below, the banks edged with slender poplars, graceful willows and little patchwork gardens. Today the huddled Arab city of Amman, capital of Trans'jor-da'nia, stands on the site of the ancient Rabbath Ammon.

"Have mercy on me, O Lord, according to Thy loving kindness;
According unto the multitude of Thy tender mercies,
    blot out my transgressions,
Wash me thoroughly from mine iniquity and
    cleanse me from my sin;
For I acknowledge my transgressions,
    and my sin is ever before me.
Create in me a clean heart, O God,
    and renew a right spirit within me.
Restore unto me the joy of Thy salvation,
    and uphold me with Thy free spirit."

But the days of David thereafter were days of disaster
and sorrow. His children quarrelled amongst themselves,
and Ab'sa-lom, his favorite son, rose up and slew his brother
and fled from the face of the king. And David suffered sore
grief for the love he bare both sons. But when he had for-
given Absalom and kissed him once again, the vain youth
prepared him chariots and horsemen and fifty men to run
before him. And he stood by the gate of Jerusalem, and to
every man that was not of the tribe of Judah, he spake
against the King, and he stole the hearts of the men of

Absalom stealing the hearts of the men of Israel. Judah and Benjamin seem very early to have felt some separation
between themselves and the other ten tribes of Israel. The men of Israel first mocked at Saul, and refused to
have him as King, while Judah and Benjamin accepted him. David was king at first only over Judah; Israel had
not acknowledged him until Saul's son was slain. Therefore, Absalom, naturally turned to the men of Israel.

Israel and went to Hebron and set himself up to reign over Israel. And there was war between David and Absalom, and David was forced to flee from Jerusalem. But when the troops were come together to battle, David commanded his captains, saying: "Deal gently for my sake with Absalom."

And there was a battle in the wood, and the servants of Absalom fled. And Absalom rode on a mule and the mule ran under the thick boughs of a great oak tree, and Absalom's head caught hold of the oak, and the mule that was under him went away, and Absalom was left hanging between the heaven and the earth. And a certain man told Joab. And Joab took three darts in his hand and thrust them through the heart of Absalom.

And David sat at the gate of the city waiting for news of the battle. And messengers came and told him that Absalom was dead. And the King went up to the chamber over the gate and wept. And he covered his face and cried with a loud voice: "Oh my son, Absalom! O Absalom, my son, my son!"

Thus Israel came again unto a union with Judah under the rule of David; but the heart of the King was sad.

Solomon the Magnificent

(ABOUT 1015-975 B.C.)

Now Bath-she'ba bare unto David in his old age a son named Solomon; and the boy was white and ruddy, the chiefest among ten thousand. His locks were black as a raven, his eyes as the eyes of doves; he was altogether lovely. Like a roe or a young hart, he leapt upon the mountains, he skipped upon the hills. He stood behind a wall, he looked forth at a window, he showed himself through the lattice.

And the lad was dear to David, tender and only beloved in the sight of Bathsheba, his mother. And the old man hoped that the life of this darling among his sons would not be like his own, full of wars, dark crimes and deep, heart-rending sorrows; but blameless, pure and peaceful, fulfilling the ideals for which he had striven in vain. And he taught the boy with care, saying: "Wisdom is the principal thing. Therefore, get wisdom, and with all thy getting, get understanding. Be thou strong and show thyself a man. And keep the commandment of the Lord, thy God."

And David promised Bathsheba to make her son king

in his stead, and he set his older sons aside, and bade men bring him Solomon. And the priest anointed the youth and set him astride the king's own mule and brought him unto the palace. And men blew trumpets before him and shouted: "God save King Solomon!"

And Solomon grew in wisdom and ruled his people with justice; for he yearned above all else for an understanding heart to discern between good and evil. And Judah and Israel dwelt safely all the days of Solomon; for the wars of David were over, the kingdom was large and peaceful; the nations round about were subdued and paying tribute, and all the tribes were one.

And Solomon grew in magnificence, mighty in glory and majesty; and he took to him wives, kings' daughters, glorious in raiment of needle work. Men sang of his bridals for ages in the beautiful *Song of Solomon*.

> Rise up, my love, my fair one, and come away;
> For lo, the winter is past, the rain is over and gone;
> The flowers appear on the earth,
> The time of the singing of birds is come.

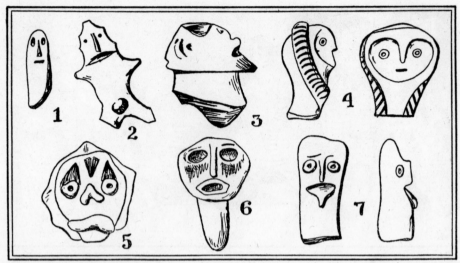

Some of the art work of Solomon's countrymen which indicates why he had to hire Phoenician workmen from Tyre to beautify the temple.   At first, the Hebrews made only bodies of men with no limbs (figure 1).   In figure 2, arms and legs are added (1000-550 B.C.).   3 adds a beard; 4 has a head-dress; 5 very remarkably, has a moustache and no beard; his moustache, his eyes, and nose are bits of clay stuck on; 6 has hollows for eyes and mouth, and grooves to represent lips; 7, is saucily sticking out her tongue, and since it has no beard, is apparently a lady!   All these figures were found at Gezer.

And Solomon set himself to build the temple. And he made a treaty with his father's friend, Hiram, King of Tyre. And Hiram sent cedars of Lebanon, and furnished cunning craftsmen to work beside Solomon's builders. And the

This figure of a Goddess is in the form of a vase ten inches high.   The mouth of the vase is in the top of the head. There is a band around the hair, with a collar around the neck, and jewelled bracelets at the wrists.   There are holes at the shoulders apparently for suspending the vessel.   Its date is just about Solomon's time (1000 B.C.) and it was found at Gezer.   The animal is also a vase, its snout forming a spout (Gezer—1000 B.C.).

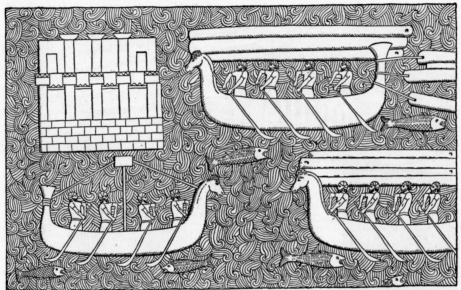

Bringing cedars from the famous cedar forests on the slopes of the Lebanon Mountains. From an Assyrian stone carving. Note the beautiful carvings of horses' heads on the prows of the boats and the fish-tails on the sterns. Boats were flat-bottomed with brows and sterns equal in height. Oars apparently had no oar-locks, but were used like poling. One boat has masts for sails. The logs are seen above the boats or dragging in the water behind. In the upper left corner rise the double lines of walls and towers that enclosed the island city of Tyre, the most important city of ancient Phoenicia. Phoenicia, with its great merchant cities of Tyre and Sidon, was the greatest trading nation of the ancient world. It lay a narrow strip of sandy coast, just north of Palestine.

pure white blocks of stone were shaped within the quarry, so there was neither hammer nor axe nor any tool of iron heard in the house while it was building.*

And the temple was built like the tabernacle, an oblong Holy Place with a smaller Holy of Holies, surrounded by chambers for priests and courts for the congregation.

And when the temple was finished, Solomon knelt before the altar and cried: "Will God indeed dwell on the earth? Behold the heaven and heaven of heavens cannot contain thee, how much less this house which I have builded. Yet hear thy people Israel when they shall pray toward this place."

*The temple was made of the glistening white stone still to be seen in Solomon's Quarries in Jerusalem; and stones have been found on the temple site today with the drippings of the paint marks of the quarrymen running upward, thus proving the Bible statement true,—the stones were all prepared and marked in the quarry so that no sound of chisel or hammer should be heard in the temple, and when they were laid some were laid with the mark upside down, which accounts for the stones found with drippings running up. Enormous difference appears between the finely squared and chiseled blocks made by Solomon's Phoenician artisans and the crude stones of David's time which were shapelessly hacked with stone tools and are still to be seen in remnants of David's wall unearthed on the Hill of Ophel.

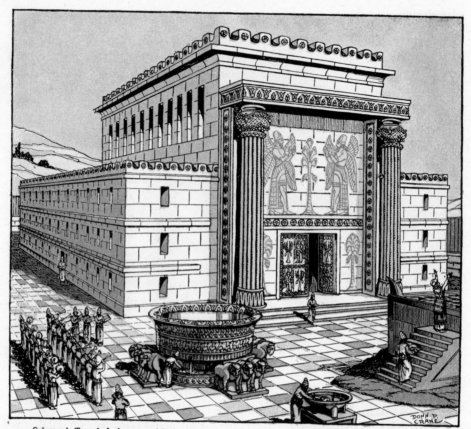

Solomon's Temple facing east with the great brazen sea resting on 12 oxen standing to the left of the picture, One of the brazen lavers on wheels is shown in the middle foreground and directly in front of the temple stands the great altar for burnt offerings with horns at its 4 corners. The altar stood on the rock crowning Mt. Moriah where tradition said Abraham took Isaac to sacrifice him and where David had built his altar on land bought from Ornan the Jebusite. This rock, carefully walled in, is still to be seen in the center of the Mosque of Omar which stands today on the site of Solomon's Temple.

There were 100 brazen lavers in the temple court and they were used for washing the animals which were to be sacrificed. Probably the great brazen sea which held 24,000 gallons of water, was a sort of reservoir holding water for general use, as very little water came up in the temple grounds.

The temple was 90 feet long x 30 wide x 45 high. It was divided like the tabernacle into 2 parts,—the small Holy of Holies (30x30 feet) and the outer Holy Place (60x30 ft.). In the Holy of Holies stood the Ark of the Covenant guarded now not only by the cherubim on its lid but by 2 standing golden cherubim who touched wings above the Ark. As in the Tabernacle, the Holy of Holies was shut off from the Holy Place by a curtain embroidered in blue and purple and scarlet. Before these curtains stood the altar of incense and the table of showbread as in the tabernacle; but there were now 10 golden candlesticks, 5 on each side of the room. The door and the walls of the temple were carved with figures of cherubim, palm trees and open flowers, and were overlaid with gold.

Against 3 sides of the temple were built rows of chambers for priests, rising in 3 tiers half way up the height of the temple and entered by winding stairs from within. Above the chambers were the "windows of narrow lights."

Before the building was a porch supported on two huge brass pillars called Jachin and Boaz. They had great bulging capitals overlaid with nets of checkerwork and draped with wreaths of chain-work from which hung scores of brazen pomegranates. The pillars were joined to the porch with a design of lilies, probably the conventional lotus lily of Egypt; for the Phoenicians who built the temple for Solomon had no original art of their own, but cleverly combined Egyptian and Assyrian models,—Egyptian lotus-lilies and Assyrian four-winged cherubim. The temple is described in I Kings, 6 and 7, and II Chronicles, 3 and 4.

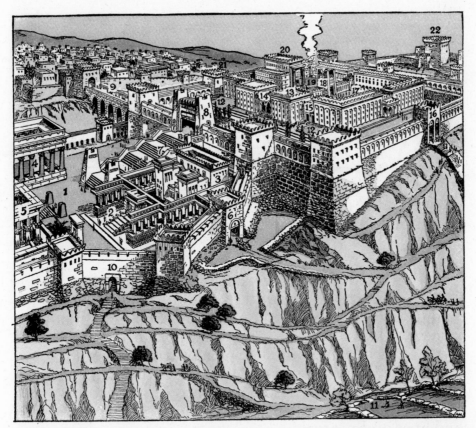

The Temple with all its courts and the connecting palace of Solomon. The public entrance to the palace was on the square marked (1). From here one entered either (2) the Porch of Judgment where stood Solomon's great throne with his private apartments behind it (3), or turned to the right into (4), the magnificent House of the Forest of Lebanon, the palace for grand public functions, built of fragrant cedar wood from the forests of Lebanon and so splendidly furnished that all its vessels were of gold and on its walls hung 300 shields of solid gold. (5) was the House of Pharaoh's Daughter, (6) was the Horse Gate "by the which the horses came into the King's house" and where Queen Ath-a-li'ah was later to be slain. (10) was the gate through which the road led down to (11) the King's Gardens, beautiful little green patches of kitchen gardens rising in terraces.

The magnificent flight of stairs marked (7) was the "ascent by which Solomon went up the House of the Lord," which so astonished the Queen of Sheba by its splendor. These steps led from the lower level of the pear-shaped Hill of O'phel where stood the Jebusite stronghold and David's ancient city, up through the palace buildings to the higher level of Mt. Moriah and the temple.

In the background the bridge of arches marked (9) led over the Valley of the Cheesemonger's, called the Ty-ro-pae'an Valley, which cut Jerusalem in two, separating Mt. Moriah from Mt. Zion. Ruins of this arch may be seen today in Jerusalem and are called from the man who discovered them, Robinson's Arch.

Entering the temple by the gate marked (8), one mounted to (12), the Court of the Gentiles beyond which foreigners were forbidden to go. To the left was the West Gate (21). In front were the Water Gate (14), the House of the High Priest (13), and the gate through which the animals were driven for sacrifice (15).

From the eastern front of the temple one entered the Court of the Gentiles by the East Gate (16), later called the Gate Beautiful and still to be seen in Jerusalem under the name of the Golden Gate. Passing a second gate one entered the Court of the Congregation (17) later called Court of the Women. In front was the High Gate or Gate of the Guard (18), passing through which one entered the Court of the Priests (19), with its brazen altar for sacrifice, and came face to face with the temple itself (20), as shown on page 182. Above the wall of the court, rose the towers of Han-an'e-el and Mea (22) fortifications of the temple. Solomon's palace is described in I Kings 7 : 1-12.

And Solomon built himself a magnificent palace, and a house for Pharaoh's daughter whom he had taken to wife. And he built up cities in the wilderness and made a navy of ships at E'lath on the Red Sea. And Hiram sent shipmen of Tyre to teach the servants of Solomon knowledge of the sea.

And the Hebrews went down to the sea in ships, and did business in great waters. And once in every three years Solomon's navy came home, bringing gold and silver, ivory and apes and peacocks.

And the king made a great throne of ivory overlaid with gold; it stood atop six steps, each guarded by golden lions.

And all King Solomon's drinking vessels were of gold, and he had shields of gold and he made silver to be in Jerusalem as stones. And he had 40,000 stalls of horses for his chariots, and twelve thousand horsemen and dromedaries. And he exceeded all the kingdoms of the earth for riches and for wisdom. And Solomon spake many proverbs and gathered into a book the proverbs of the land.

Now when the queen of Sheba heard of the fame of Solomon, she came to prove him with hard questions, and she came with a very great train, with camels that bare spices and gold and precious stones. And she communed with Solomon of all that was in her heart. And Solomon answered all her questions. And when she had seen all Solomon's wisdom and the house that he had built, and the meat of his table, and the sitting of his servants, and the attendance of his ministers, and their apparel, and his cupbearers, and his ascent by which he went up to the house of the Lord, there was no more spirit in her. And she said to the King: "It was a true report that I heard in mine own land of thine acts and of thy wisdom. Behold, the half was not told me."

And she gave the king an hundred and twenty talents of gold and of spices very great store, and precious stones. And King Solomon gave unto her whatsoever she asked of his royal bounty. So she turned and went back to Sheba.

But it came to pass when Solomon was old that his heart was no longer perfect with the Lord his God. His too-much splendor undid him, and he loved many strange women of the Moabites, of the Ammonites, of the Edomites, and the Hittites, and he sacrificed to their gods, to Ash'to-reth, the goddess of the Phoenicians, to Che'mosh, the abomination of Moab, and to Mo'lech, the abomination of Ammon.

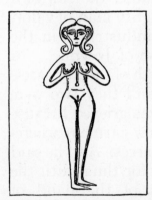

A figure of Ashtoreth made about Solomon's time and found at Gezer. As the nourishing earth-mother, Ashtoreth always offers her breasts to feed the world. She is a symbol of mere material growth and sustenance. Therefore her worship was gross feasting and junketing. See the vase, page 180, also page 241.

An ancient figure of Mo'lech from a private museum in Jaffa. Mo'lech was the cruel and blood-thirsty god of the Ammonites. It was to him that the Hebrews so insistently offered human sacrifice. "They made their sons and their daughters to pass through the fire unto Molech," the Bible frequently says.

A-hi'jah the prophet rends his garment in twelve pieces and gives ten pieces to Jeroboam, to signify that ten tribes of Israel will separate from the two tribes of Judah and Benjamin and make Jeroboam King of Israel.

Moreover Solomon oppressed Israel with governors and tax-gatherers, but his own tribe of Judah he oppressed not.

And it came to pass as Solomon was repairing the wall of Jerusalem that he looked on a certain young man born of the tribe of Ephraim, Jer'o-bo'am by name, the son of a widow woman. And Jeroboam was a mighty man of valor, and Solomon seeing him, that he was industrious in the work, made him ruler over all the house of Joseph.

But it chanced that Jeroboam went forth of the city gates. And the prophet, A-hi'jah, met him; and they two were alone in the field. And Ahijah's heart was grieved because of the sins of Solomon; so he took the new garment wherewith he was clad and rent it into twelve pieces. And he said unto Jeroboam: "Take thee ten pieces; for thus saith the Lord: 'I will rend the kingdom out of the hand of Solomon and give ten tribes to thee.'"

And when Solomon heard what Ahijah had done he sought to kill Jeroboam; but Jeroboam fled unto Shi'shak, King of Egypt, and was there until Solomon died.

VII

The Divided Kingdoms
Israel and Judah
(965-586 B. C.)

Now Solomon died, and the men of Israel came unto his son, Re-ho-bo'am, at Shechem, saying: "Thy father made our yoke grievous. Lighten thou our service."

Then Rehoboam asked counsel of the old men, Solomon's counsellors, and they said: "Lighten their yoke."

But Rehoboam consulted the young men, which had grown up with him, and they said: "Say to this people, 'I will add to your yoke. My father chastised you with whips, but I will chastise you with scorpions!'"

And the King answered the people thus roughly. Therefore ten tribes revolted and called Jeroboam home from Egypt to be their king. And they stoned Rehoboam's tax-gatherer; and Rehoboam fled from Shechem.

So Israel rebelled against the house of David.

Henceforth there were two Hebrew kingdoms, Judah to the south and Israel to the north. And Rehoboam had war continually, war with Jeroboam and with Shi'shak, King of Egypt.

The men of Israel stone Rehoboam's tax-gatherer and revolt from Judah. Rehoboam flees in his chariot from Shechem which city later became Jeroboam's seat of government.

Rehoboam being led a captive to Shishak (or She'shonk), from Shishak's sculpture at Kar'nak, which records his victories (926 B.C.). The hieroglyphics read: "Kingdom of Judah." This sculpture also contains the first historical mention of Abraham, 1200 years after his time, in listing among conquered cities, "the Field of Abraham." See Vol. I, p. 246.

And Jeroboam feared lest the hearts of his people should return unto Rehoboam, if they went up year by year to do sacrifice in the House of the Lord at Jerusalem. So he made two calves of gold and set them up as gods, the one in Bethel, the other in Dan.

Thus Jeroboam did evil, and there fell on Israel days of confusion and inner revolt; for one Ba'a-sha slew Jeroboam's son and all his line; and Zimri slew Baasha's son as he drank himself drunk in Tirzah; and Omri, Captain of the Host, laid siege to Zimri, till Zimri set his own palace afire and burned himself within it.

Then Omri reigned and brought order in Israel. And Omri bought the hill of Samaria and made his capital there. And all these kings of Israel worshipped the golden calves; but Asa, king of Judah, and Je-hosh'a-phat his son, lived righteously and justly.

And Judah and Israel both were exceedingly little nations, compared with the might and glory of Egypt and Assyria.

Judah, the southern kingdom, was a race of highland shepherds, dwelling on stony hills. Perched amid her mountains, Judah sat as an eagle, beholding the nations of earth, their glory and their

Historical mention of Jeroboam in a seal discovered at Megiddo. The seal reads "Shema, servant of Jeroboam." Jeroboam's fear of Rehoboam led him to introduce idolatry into Israel to keep people from going to worship at Jerusalem.

The gate of Samaria, where ruins of the palace built by Omri and Ahab, may still be seen today. Samaria, the capital of Northern Israel, rose on a beautifully rounded hill, 330 feet above a rolling plain.

splendor, but shut off from them all by her girdle of rocky hills. Therefore the people of Judah held more securely to God and their own old native customs.

Israel, on the contrary, the northernmost of the kingdoms, was open, fair, and smiling, a place of gentle mountain slopes and green and fertile valleys. Israel was more warlike, more of a trading nation, more open to foreign influence; for Israel's stretch of seacoast was then the world's great war-path, over which Assyria went marching to the southward, and Egypt to the northward, whenever the two great rivals would meet and fly at each other's throats.

Israel and Philistia, the bridge between Egypt and Assyria, with Syria the buffer-state, holding Assyria back from Israel. Judah with no sea-coast, alone in her mountains, a little strip of land only 55 miles long by 25 miles broad.

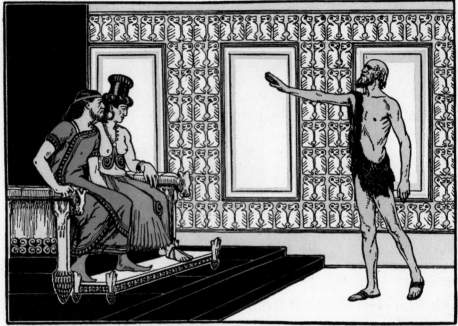

Elijah suddenly appears before Ahab and Jezebel in their ivory-panelled palace.   The bird figures in ivory panel-
ling on the wall were discovered at Gezer.   Such were the ivory palaces of Ahab and of Jeroboam II. The costume
of Jezebel is taken from the little Phoenician statue on page 192.

Elijah, the Fiery Prophet, the Champion of Jehovah

(ABOUT 875 B.C.)

Now it came to pass in process of time that Ahab, the son
of Omri, reigned over Israel. And Ahab loved splendor, and
he built cities and made him an ivory palace. And he held
Moab under with a heavy hand, and he yearned to make
Israel great as Solomon had in his day. Nevertheless, Ahab
did evil more than all who went before him. For he took to
wife Jez′e-bel, daughter of Eth′ba′al, king of Tyre, and she
stirred him up to wickedness. And he reared an altar in
Samaria to Mel′kart the sun-god, the Tyrian Baal. And
Ahab and Jezebel made the worship of Baal, with all its
evil rites, the state religion of Israel. And Jezebel took the

prophets of Jehovah, men who dwelt together in guilds seeking to know the will of God, and she had them, every one, slain, save only for an hundred that a good man hid in a cave and fed with bread and water. But the 450 prophets of Baal, Jezebel took to the palace to eat at her own table.

And there was kindled a flame in the heart of Elijah, the Tishbite, where he dwelt on the east of Jordan mid the stony mountains of Gil'e-ad; for he saw that the time was come when Israel must choose—would she serve God or Baal?

On a sudden Elijah came down from his mountains, startling in his abruptness, and he stood before Ahab with unshorn locks and a girdle of goatskin about his loins, a figure austere but majestic. And he said: "Because of what thou hast done, there shall be neither rain nor dew in Israel."

Elijah in the days of famine and drought, alone in the deep ravine cut by the torrent of the brook Cherith, I Kings, 17:5. Background copied from a photograph. Such wild and desolate scenes are characteristic of the mountain land that formed the southern kingdom of Judah. The Bible story says that ravens fed Elijah here during the long days of famine.

And there fell a great drought on the land and Elijah went and hid himself in the rocky ravine of the Che'rith. And there he dwelt alone, depending solely on God to provide him with food and drink.

And Ahab went out in search of a little grass to keep his horses and mules. And he saw Elijah coming, and cried in bitter reproach: "Art thou he that troubleth Israel?"

But Elijah answered: "I have not troubled Israel; but thou and thy father's house. Ye have caused this drought."

Then Elijah put forth a challenge unto the prophets of Baal to meet him on Mount Carmel.

"Let each lay a bullock on wood and put no fire under," he said, "and call ye on your gods and I will call on the Lord. And the God that answers by fire, let him be acknowledged as God."

Now Ahab dwelt in Jez're-el more than he did in Samaria; and south of the Plain of Jezreel the rocky nose of Mt.

Carmel plunges into the sea. So Ahab went up from Jezreel to look on the contest at Carmel. And the priests of Baal prepared their bullock in sight of all the people, and they stood, four hundred and fifty strong, against the one prophet of God.

And Elijah cried to the throng: "How long halt ye between two opinions? If the Lord be God, follow him; but if Baal, then follow him."

And the people answered him not a word.

A Phoenician priestess or goddess in such garb as Jezebel may have worn. Note the ancient pendant, tall cap and earrings. Found at Tortose in Phoenicia and now in the Louvre.

An ancient Phoenician Baal or god, with typical belt and helmet. Baal was the Phoenician word for Lord, and is often found in the plural, Baalim or Baals, meaning gods. Found at Tortose in Phoenicia.

Before their altar on Mt. Carmel, the priests of Baal in a frenzy beg their god to send fire.   Elijah calmly looks on.

Then the priests of Baal called on their god and begged him to send them fire from morning until noon. But there was no voice that answered. And the prophets of Baal grew anxious; for all the people were looking. And they leapt about their altar crying aloud and shouting.

And at noon Elijah mocked and said: "Cry louder; for thy god is busy talking; or he is gone a-hunting; or peradventure he sleepeth and needeth to be awaked."

And when they heard his taunts, the prophets of Baal were frantic. They leapt and cried and cut themselves with knives, till the blood gushed out upon them; but there came no fire to their altar.

And at evening Elijah made ready his bullock and soaked it with water and spake one simple prayer: "Hear me, O Lord! Hear me, that this people may know thou art God in Israel, the one Lord God in Israel!"

And the fire fell and the flames leapt up and consumed the sacrifice. And the people fell on their faces crying: "The Lord He is the God!"

And they slew the prophets of Baal.

Ahab racing madly with the storm and Elijah running before him. Behind rises the rocky headland of Mt. Carmel-by-the-sea, the most prominent feature of Israel's coast-line. The two race toward the Plain of Jezreel.

Then Elijah said to Ahab: "Eat and drink; for now the drought is broken. At last there cometh rain."

So Ahab sat down to eat; and Elijah went up Mount Carmel and cast himself on the earth with his face between his knees. And he said to his servant: "Look to the sea!"

And his servant said: "I see nothing!" And seven times the servant looked, when behold, there rose out of the sea, a little cloud, no bigger than a man's hand. And Elijah said: "Go unto Ahab and say, 'Haste thee away to shelter.'"

Soon the heaven was black with clouds, heavy with wind and rain. And Ahab dashed in his chariot madly across the plain, fleeing before the storm. And Elijah drew tighter his goatskin and ran before him to Jezreel.

Thus, for a little time, the people acknowledged God and rain refreshed the land; but Jezebel sent to Elijah, saying: "So let the gods do to me, and more also, if I have not thy life by tomorrow about this time."

And they who had shouted for God returned again unto Baal.

And Elijah arose and fled to the wilderness. And he sat down under a juniper tree and wished that he might die; for he felt that he stood alone with every hand against him.

And he journeyed into the desert even unto Mount Horeb and dwelt there in a cave.

And there came a great strong wind, an earthquake, and flaming fire; but Elijah knew that God was in no such ways of destruction. And lastly there came a still small voice that spoke to Elijah's heart, and that was the voice of God.

And Elijah was comforted of God and it was revealed to him that there still remained in Israel 7,000 faithful ones who would not bow the knee to Baal. And he rose up to return, saying: "The house of Ahab must fall if knowledge of God shall continue to live in Israel."

And he came on Elisha, a young man ploughing a field with twelve yoke of oxen before him. And he cast his mantle on Elisha; and Elisha left the oxen and kissed his father and mother and hasted to follow Elijah.

Elijah casts his mantle on Elisha as he is ploughing. The same simple type of plow is still used in Palestine.

Assyria now begins to loom up as the rival of Egypt and the terror of Israel. The first Assyrian King to cross the Euphrates was Ashur-natsir-pal (878 B.C.)   The king with his chariot and officers is in the boat. (See page 58.)

Now Ahab had two powerful enemies, Ben'ha'dad, king of Syria, who was ever seizing more land on the northern border of Israel; and Shal'man-e'ser III, the ambitious king of Assyria.   And Ahab made one of a league that defeated Shalmaneser, and he smote Benhadad of Syria in one campaign in the hills and one campaign in the valleys.

And Ahab was puffed up with pride.   And there was one, Na'both, a poor man of Jezreel that had a vineyard hard by the palace.   And Ahab desired the vineyard that he might make there a garden.   And he offered to buy the place; but Naboth loved his home and he would not sell it to Ahab.

And Ahab came to his palace, heavy and displeased. And he lay down on his bed and sulked and would not eat.

And Jezebel said: "Why is thy spirit so sad?"

And Ahab said: "Because Naboth will not give me his vineyard."

And Jezebel said: "Dost thou now rule in Israel?   Arise! Eat bread and be merry.   I will give thee the vineyard."

Then she wrote letters in Ahab's name and sealed them with his seal, saying: "Proclaim a feast and send two lying rascals to cry against Naboth, saying: 'Thou didst blaspheme God and the king.'   And stone Naboth till he die."

So they to whom she had written hired two lying rascals to come and accuse Naboth falsely; and they carried him forth of the city, and stoned him till he died.

And Jezebel said unto Ahab: "Arise! Take possession of the vineyard; for Naboth is dead."

And Ahab rose up to go; but Elijah stood in his path.

"Thou hast done evil." Elijah cried: "Behold where dogs lick Naboth's blood, there shall they lick thy blood. Dogs shall eat Jezebel, and thy house shall not endure."

Then Ahab rent his clothes and put sackcloth upon his flesh. Nevertheless, in three years time, he went forth again to battle; for he had made a league with Je-hosh'a-phat, King of Judah, the first tie of friendship in many years between the two Hebrew kingdoms.

And the two went up together against the king of Syria, even to Ra'moth-gil'e-ad.

Now the king of Syria commanded his captains saying: "Fight with none save Ahab." But Ahab disguised himself; so the captains followed Jehoshaphat in all his royal robes. Howbeit, a man drew a bow at a venture and smote Ahab, not knowing that he was king.

Wherefore Ahab said to his charioteer: "Carry me out of the host; for I am sore wounded."

And the battle increased; and the king propped himself up in his chariot, until the

A typical Syrian with a narrow pointed beard, from an Egyptian carving. In the early days of Egypt, Syrians, Canaanites, and Hebrews are all called Syrians on the monuments; but gradually Aramaeans, a different race of Semites, pushed their way up from Arabia, and settled in Syria, their chief kingdom being Damascus.

These people were, for centuries the enemies of the Jews; yet they were little more powerful than the Jews themselves before the might of Egypt and Assyria. The wisest Hebrew rulers saw how foolhardy it would be to wipe out Syria wholly, because she lay as a buffer-state, the only effective barrier to hold Assyria back from Israel. (See map, page 189.)

For this reason Ahab, though he conquered Ben-hadad of Syria, did not crush him wholly but made a treaty with him and fought by his side against Shal-maneser III of Assyria.

even; but about the time of the sun-going-down, he died.

And his chariot came to Samaria covered with his blood, and one washed it in the pool, and dogs licked up his blood even as Elijah had said.

And A'ha-zi'ah, son of Ahab, reigned but two years in Israel; for he fell down through a lattice in his upper chamber and died, and Jehoram, his brother, was king. And Jehoram put away the Baals; but he clave to the golden calves; and Jezebel, his mother, still remained a dark and sombre figure of evil at his court.

Then Elijah crossed over Jordan, and Elisha went over with him. And fifty from the guild of the prophets, in their robes of camel's hair, stood on the hills afar off. And as the two walked together, the fiery spirit of Elijah passed away from earth. And Elisha beheld as it were, a vision attuned to that spirit—a chariot of fire and horses of fire, and Elijah going up by a whirlwind unto heaven.

Thus the breath of cleansing, that had dwelt in the heart of Elijah, that burning, glowing flame, alive with a confident sense of the power and glory of God, vanished forever from earth.

And Elisha picked up the mantle of Elijah; and the sons of the prophets said: "The spirit of Elijah doth rest on Elisha."

And Elisha went his way to carry on the work of Elijah; to declare one God alone, and the service of God in righteousness and the justice of man to man.

And Jehoram hated Elisha and sent his men to kill him; but Elisha dwelt in safety among the guild of the prophets.

And when it was heard that Ahab was dead, the nations round about which had paid tribute to Israel in the days of David and Solomon, grew restive and rebelled.

And Me'sha, king of Moab, rebelled; for Mesha was a sheep-master and rendered unto Ahab 100,000 lambs and

100,000 rams as yearly tribute. And Jehoram made a league with Jehoshaphat, and with the king of Edom and they went to fight against Mesha.

And the Moabites gathered together all that could put on armor and hasted to the border to meet the Children of Israel; but the Children of Israel put them to flight. They beat down their cities, cast stones on their fields, stopped all their wells of water and went forward smiting the foe, till the Moabites shut themselves up within the strong walls of Kir.

And the city of Kir of Moab, high on a lofty hill shaped like a great triangle, lifted its strong-walled battlements sheer from a deep ravine. Save for a single gate on a narrow neck of land that connected the gorge-girt triangle with the tall hills round about, the only way into that stronghold was through four rock-hewn tunnels closed with heavy doors.

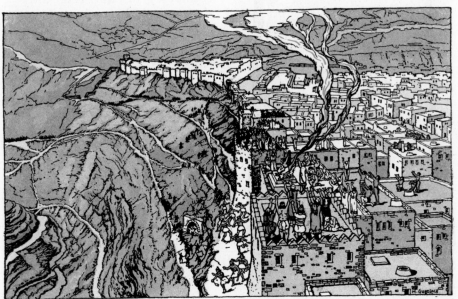

Mesha offers his eldest son as a sacrifice on the walls of Kir of Moab, the strong fortress on a gorge-girt hill, which except for a single gate on the narrow neck of land to the left had no other entrance but tunnels.

But, strong as the city was, the Israelites besieged Kir, surrounding it with slingers. And when Mesha, King of Moab, saw the battle sore against him, he took seven hundred men and tried to break a way through to go to the King of Edom; but the enemy threw him back; and then as a last resort, to buy the help of his god, Mesha took his eldest son that should have reigned in his stead, and, following ancient custom, he offered him to Che'mosh, burning him on the walls in sight of all the foe. Beholding such a sacrifice, the Hebrews fled in terror; and Mesha was left victorious, to carve these boastful words on a monument of black stone:

I am Mesha, son of Che'mosh-me'lech, King of Moab, the Di'bonite;

My father reigned over Moab for thirty years and reign did

I after my father. And I have made this high place for Chemosh in Kir,

Because he saved me from all the kings, and because he let me see my pleasure on all that hated me.

Omri was king of Israel and he afflicted Moab many days because Chemosh was angry with his land,

And his son succeeded him; and he also said: "I will afflict Moab." In my days he spake thus.

But I saw my pleasure on him and on his house, and Israel perished with everlasting destruction.

The famous Moabite stone of black basalt, found at Dibon in Moab in 1868. It records Mesha's own story of his wars with Ahab and Omri, and was engraved at the command of one who actually met these old Bible Kings face to face. The names are in nearly every case identical with those in the Bible. The stone is one of the most interesting monuments ever discovered in corroborating the Bible stories.

Now Jehoshaphat of Judah, married his son to Ahab's daughter, Ath-a-li′ah. And Athaliah was evil, like Jezebel her mother. She stirred up her husband and A′ha-zi′ah, her son, to rear altars to Baal in Judah and depart from all the good ways of Jehoshaphat and Asa.

And Ahaziah made a league with his uncle, Jehoram of Israel, and they went together to battle with Haz′a-el, King of Syria. And the Syrians wounded Jehoram and he returned to Jezreel. And Ahaziah came to visit him.

Then Elisha saw that the time was ripe to fulfill the plan of Elijah and wipe out the house of Ahab, idolators and tyrants. So he sent a young man of the prophets unto a captain of the host, one Je′hu, at Ramoth-gilead. And the young man found the captains sitting together in camp. And he called Jehu apart, to come in unto an house and there he anointed him king. Then he opened the door and fled. And when Jehu came forth again, the other captains said: "Wherefore came that mad fellow to thee?"

And Jehu made answer: "He came to anoint me King."

The captains greet Jehu as King before the city of Ramoth-gilead where they are encamped against the Syrians.

Jehu drives furiously across the plain toward the city of Jezreel. Background from a photograph of Jezreel.

Then the captains hasted and took every man his garment and laid it under Jehu's feet on the stairs. And they blew the trumpets, saying: "Jehu is king." And Jehu set out in a chariot driving furiously to Jezreel. And there stood a watchman on the tower in Jezreel and he spied the company of Jehu coming. And he said: "The driving is like the driving of Jehu, son of Nimshi, for he driveth furiously."

And Jehoram said: "Send an horseman to meet them and let him say: 'Is there peace in Ramoth-gilead?' "

But three horsemen who went forth joined themselves unto Jehu. Then Jehoram called for his chariot, and Ahaziah went with him. And they sallied forth and met Jehu in the gardens of Naboth's Vineyard.

And Jehoram said unto Jehu: "Is there peace, Jehu?"

And Jehu answered: "What peace, so long as the sins of thy mother Jezebel and her witchcrafts are so many?"

And Jehoram fled, crying to Ahaziah: "There is treachery!"

And Jehu drew bow with full strength and smote Jehoram through the heart; and he sank down in his chariot. And Jehu had his body cast into Naboth's Vineyard.

And Ahaziah turned to flee by way of the garden house; but Jehu followed after him, crying: "Smite him also!" And they slew him at the ascent of Gur.

And Jezebel heard what was come to pass, and she painted her face and tired her head and looked out at a window, and as Jehu entered the gate, she mocked and said: "Greetings, O Zimri, thy master's murderer!"

And Jehu looked up, saying: "Who is on my side?"

And there looked out to him two eunuchs and he said: "Throw her down!" So they threw Jezebel down, and Jehu trod her under foot of his horses and his chariot. And when he was come to the palace he said: "Go, bury this accursed woman." But they found no more of her than bones; for dogs had eaten her flesh, as Elijah had foretold.

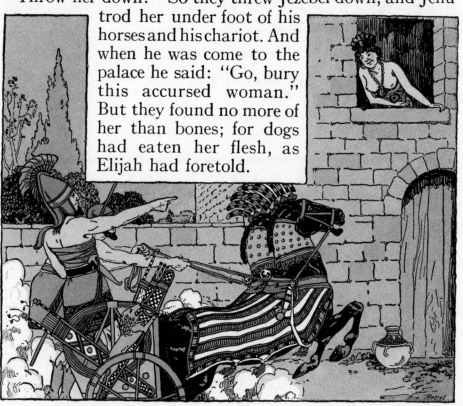

Shalmaneser's own record of Jehu's tribute from the famous black obelisk of Shalmaneser III. Shalmaneser, under protection of the winged sun-disk, stands beneath his parasol followed by two attendants. Jehu kisses the ground before him. Jehu's submission to Assyria foretold the years of struggle ahead of Judah and Israel. (Page 66.)

Then Jehu slew the worshippers of Baal, and brake his altars and destroyed Baal out of Israel. And he kissed the

The Hebrews in this picture are bearing buckets and goblets of gold. The last two bear long strips of lead. Note the peculiar cap worn by the Hebrews. This is a true story of Jehu, carved from life. Jehu bought the support of Assyria to help him hold the throne he had seized. The Black Obelisk is now in the British Museum.

Four Assyrian officials follow Jehu, then come thirteen Hebrews bearing gifts and tribute. The three in this picture bear bags of gold. The Hebrews are making submission to the cruelest and most tyrannical power of the ancient world, an enemy that exulted in impaling men on poles or building pyramids of human heads. (Page 60.)

ground before Shalmaneser III, the ambitious King of Assyria, and bought his support with the payment of tribute.

The first bearers here carry well-filled packages on their shoulders, the next two carry cups with handles and bear some articles, rich garments, perhaps, on their shoulders; the last has a tray of valuables on his head. All the Hebrews wear boots; the Assyrians wear sandals. Hebrew robes are less elaborately fringed than the Assyrians'.

And now there remained of the evil line of Ahab only Ath-a-li'ah, the wicked queen-mother of Judah; and when Athaliah heard that Ahaziah was dead, she slew all his sons and made herself queen in his stead. But Je-hosh'e-ba, sister of Ahaziah, stole one little yearling babe, even Jo'ash, son of the king, and she hid him and his nurse in a bedchamber during the time of the murder. Then she took the babe to the temple unto her husband, Je-hoi'a-da, the High Priest, and there the child dwelt in secret.

And Athaliah reigned for six years over the land. But when Joash was seven years old, Jehoiada sent and fetched the rulers over hundreds, and the captains, and the guards, and he stationed them as a guard from the right corner of the court of the temple even unto the left corner; and he brought forth the boy and showed him to the people. And they put the crown on his head and anointed him and clapped their hands and said: "God save the King."

And Athaliah heard the noise, and she came to the temple. And when she looked, behold, the King stood by a pillar of the door, and the princes and the trumpeters stood by him and all the people rejoiced and blew with trumpets. And Athaliah rent her clothes and cried: "Treason! Treason!"

Jehosheba, sister of Ahaziah, saves the little baby Joash from the massacre of the King's children ordered by their grandmother, the wicked queen Athaliah. On the wall hangs a calendar of the period found at Beth-palet.

The boy, Joash, seven years old, is proclaimed King in the court of the temple. Athaliah, at sight of what has occurred, rends her clothes in despair. Joash ruled in justice so long as Jehoiada lived.

But Jehoiada, the priest, commanded the captains and the officers, saying: "Take her forth and slay her."

And they laid hands on her and took her to the Horse Gate of the palace, and there they slew her. And the people went to the house of Baal that Athaliah had made, and brake it down with its altars and its images. And they built up the temple of God.

Thus ended, both in Judah and in Israel, the long struggle of Elijah and Elisha with the house of Ahab and Jezebel, and the evil worship of Baal. Their work was to stand as champions for Jehovah, the one God of Israel, a God of justice and righteousness, and to prove His mighty power against the degrading beliefs of the nations round about.

A silver dipper in the form of a swimming girl found at Beth'-pa'let in Palestine. A beautiful article made in this rich and flourishing time and one of the few treasures of the Hebrew monarchy ever found.

Amos the Herdsman, a Prophet to Northern Israel

Now Jer-o-bo'am II, great grandson of Jehu, sat on the throne of Israel, grand monarch of days of success, ruling prosperously and long. He warred with Syria, Israel's chief enemy for many a generation; and he took Damascus, her capital city, and all she had conquered in times past of the ancient dominion of Israel. He brought back Ammon and Moab under the rule of Israel, and his lords and ladies dwelt splendidly, having summer-houses and winter-houses, and houses of fine hewn stone paneled in richest ivory. They lolled on beds of ivory—feasting, drinking, singing, while the poor, in sullen misery, starved or were sold as slaves.

But all unnoted in Israel, a dark cloud was looming to eastward—Assyria, the merciless, was ever drawing nearer, striking her blows at Syria in constant succession of wars. And when the day should come that Syria bowed the neck, no barrier would be left to keep the Assyrian wolf from springing at Judah and Israel. Israel was all puffed up in that last height of foolish power that comes before a fall.

Men said they were true to God because they sent streams of offerings to the altars of Bethel and Gilgal; but the golden calves set up there by Jeroboam I, and honestly meant by him as simple signs of God, representing His strength and power, had grown to be gods themselves in the eyes of the foolish people. It was to the golden calves their offerings were made.

And the people said: "Elijah hath proved to us that Jehovah is God of Israel. He will surely make us glorious if only we send him offerings. The day of the Lord will come, a day of crowning victory, when He will set Israel up above all the nations of earth."

And they went on oppressing and feasting.

Now there dwelt in those days in the little town of Te-ko'a in the wilderness of Judah, one Amos, an herdsman and pruner of sycamore trees. And Tekoa stood on an hill at the very edge of the desert, a place of thistles and prickly bushes and quickly fading flowers. From the height of Tekoa, Amos could look through clefts in the desolate range of mountains to the land of breathless stillness above the far Dead Sea. A simple fellow was Amos, rough, austere, and rugged. His comrades were herdsmen and reapers, ploughmen and treaders of grapes; and the daily sights he

The rough, strong herdsman, Amos, and his daily comrades, the husbandmen, looking across the desolate wilderness of Tekoa to the distant Dead Sea in whose salty waters no living thing could exist.

saw were wandering flocks of sheep, husbandmen sifting corn in a sieve, yokes of oxen ploughing, and carts pressed down with sheaves. Often in that solitude he heard the roars of lions, or rescued a lamb from a bear.

But, far though Amos lived from the world, he followed with fervent interest all that went on in Israel, the course of the Syrian wars, the awful threat of Assyria, the tyranny of the rich, the suffering of the poor. And he felt the wrongs of the poor; for he himself was poor, and there burned in his heart a passion, a fiery love for justice.

And as Amos followed his flock, he felt that he heard the voice of God roaring forth in judgment, while all around were deaf, asleep in slothful ease. He went to blow a trumpet to waken silly Israel out of her deathlike sleep.

Stern, uncouth, and rough, no member of the prophet's guild which had long been established at Bethel, an unknown shepherd from Judah, he went to preach in Israel, to face grandees and princes, priests, professional prophets, and a multitude of pilgrims at the king's own splendid shrine, at Bethel, the magnificent, chief seat of the golden calf.

Suddenly he appeared, clad in his coarse, shaggy sheepskin, and he spoke with force and fire.

"Thus saith the Lord, 'For three transgressions of Syria and for four I will not turn away the punishment!'"

Hearers drew near to listen. Syria was their enemy; they liked to hear her decried. Had he first spoken of Israel, the Israelites would have mobbed him. Then he denounced Philistia, Ammon, Moab, Judah. But when he had gathered his crowd by condemning Israel's foes, Amos startled them all with striking straight at Israel.

"Israel," he cried, "thinketh she hath security because the Lord is her God. But the Lord is not her God alone. He brought her out from Egypt; but likewise it was He who brought the Philistines from Crete, and governs all

The people were shouting that the day of the Lord would be a day of mighty victory for Israel. Amos alone understood that, unless his people ceased their licentiousness and oppression, the day of the Lord would be a day of dark defeat. He dared to preach to princes at Bethel. (The great stone of this stony land is from a photograph).

the peoples. He maketh no difference between the Children of Israel and the black men of E'thi-o'pi-a who dwell in the ends of the earth. All are responsible unto God for leading lives of goodness; and Judah and Israel He holdeth responsible above all nations of earth because to them hath been revealed more of His real nature. Therefore since they break His laws, their punishment will be greater.

"Woe unto you," he cried, "that desire the day of the Lord! The day of the Lord shall be to you darkness and not light. Thus saith the Lord: 'Woe to them that are at ease in Zion, that lie upon beds of ivory and chant to the sound of the viol. Ye have sold the righteous for silver and the poor for a pair of shoes.' Hear this word of the Lord. 'Ye shall go captive with the first that go captive.' Ye think God is your God alone. He is God of all the earth. Lo, He that formeth the mountains and createth the wind and declareth unto man what is His thought, that is the Lord, the God of Hosts. Seek good and not evil that ye may live. So the Lord shall be with you!"

The people listened aghast. How dared the fellow speak so, the rough, uncouth, beggarly rascal, speaking to grandees and princes. He spake to them roughly, too. He called them kine of Ba'shan, called the grandees cattle! He said in the day of battle they would run away like cows! Their anger grew ever greater. And at last he dared to say: "Jeroboam shall die by the sword and Israel shall be led away captive out of the land."

Then there was an uproar, and cries of "Treason!" against him. And Am'a-zi'ah, the high priest, sent in haste unto Jeroboam, saying: "Amos conspires against thee."

And unto Amos he cried: "O thou seer, go away! Go back to your own land Judah! Earn your bread with your prophecies there! But prophesy not again any more at Bethel; for it is the king's chapel; it is the king's court!"

Then answered Amos and said: "I am no professional prophet. I prophesy not for bread. I am an herdsman and dresser of sycamore trees. I prophesy because the Lord hath sent me; and what I say is true. Israel shall go captive! Your sons and daughters shall fall by the sword, and you yourself shall be carried off to die in a foreign land!"

And with these words he vanished, a prophet of one appearing. For he returned to the wilderness and wrote his prophecies down since the people refused to hearken, becoming thus the first prophet to leave a written record.

And as he pondered alone in the silence of the hills, he saw a ray of hope. God would sift his people as husbandmen sift their grain, destroying the chaff but leaving the wheat. God would sift out the evil and leave a remnant rich in goodness, to make a better Israel.

Elijah had proved that God was the one and only God, the God of Israel. Amos added that God was God of all the earth, a God who demanded not sacrifice, but that men should live together in righteousness and justice.

Hosea, the Prophet of Love
(NORTHERN ISRAEL, ABOUT 750-725 B.C.)

Some years after Amos appeared, there dwelt in Israel a man named Ho-se'a, with Go'mer his wife, and two small sons and a daughter.

Hosea was a tender father, a man of strong affections, warm and very loving. He taught his children to walk, taking them by their arms or holding them up with cords. He loved the clean breath of the wind blowing up from the wilderness, the tender refreshment of rain reviving the drooping wheat fields and the early dew on the grass that passeth away so quickly. He watched with joy the flight of birds and the morning clouds skimming swiftly over the clear blue sky.

But Gomer was not such a woman as Hosea was a man. Gomer loved to wear pendants and bracelets, anklets, and earrings, and chains. It was not a woman like Gomer who could understand and rejoice in the great, loving heart of her husband. Gomer preferred to go mincingly,

Hosea, who learned the meaning of love through being a tender father, and Gomer, his proud, faithless wife. Hosea lived after Amos in the latter part of the prosperous reign of Jeroboam II of Israel.

Hosea attacks the High Place by showing the people his children.   The girl he has named No-Mercy, and the smallest boy Not-My-People, to warn the folk that God will show no mercy to Israel nor recognize them as his people if they persist in evil.   But in his own home Hosea's warm heart would not let him use these harsh names. There with affectionate tenderness, he called his little girl Mercy and his little boy My-People.   (Hosea 2:1).

In the ancient days of Canaan, each town had its High Place or hill-top sacred to the worship of Baal, the god who possessed the soil, and to As-tar'te, the goddess of fertility.   The wooden pole or A-she'rah which the woman is wreathing with flowers represented the evergreen tree which was sacred to Astarte, and the tall stone pillar or Mazzebah represented the male god Baal.   (See the remains of the High Place of Gezer, page 340.)

When the Hebrews settled in Canaan they took over these High Places almost without change, and worshipped Jehovah there with all the old heathen rites that had once belonged to Baal; yet Hosea was the first of the prophets to say distinctly that worshipping God in such a manner was one of the foremost causes of Israel's sins.

Hosea said "The High Places, the sin of Israel shall be destroyed.   Thou shalt call God no more Baali (the Canaanite word for Lord and husband), but Ishii (the Israelite word for Lord and husband) that is: Call God no more the mere source of material life, but Lord and husband in the highest sense of the word, meaning one who gives love and protection and supplies every need."   Such a husband Hosea himself longed to be.

looking for other lovers. And she decked herself in her earrings and jewels and went away after her lovers, forgetting her little children and leaving Hosea alone. And the heart of Hosea was heavy and he said to his eldest son: "Say to your brother and sister, 'Plead with your mother, plead, that she may come home again.' "

But Gomer would not come home, and Hosea was left alone to be mother and father both, unto his three young

children. Deep were his grief and anger. He passed through
bitter days when he cried in his anguish and rage: "Would
I could strip Gomer naked and set her forth for a show as
in the day she was born!"

But out of that fearful struggle, he rose still more
warmly loving, more tenderly forgiving, longing again to
hear Gomer singing about the house as in the days of her
youth.

And in his sorrow, Hosea saw that Israel was faithless to
God, as his wife had been faithless to him. As Gomer had
sinned because she did not really know the great loving
heart of her husband; so Israel had sinned because she
knew not the great loving heart of God. And just as he was
ready to forgive his erring wife, so was God ready to forgive
His erring people, if they would return unto Him.

The golden calves of Bethel, the wanton Baals of the high
places, those were Israel's lovers; God was her deserted

Hosea buys back his faithless wife who is offered for sale as a slave. Thereby he learns the meaning of forgiveness
and adds to man's knowledge of God, the fact that God loves and redeems mankind as Hosea has redeemed and
loved Gomer. Hosea is not to be confused with Hoshea, the last king of Israel. They are two different men.

husband. And Hosea cried to the people: "Israel has forgotten his maker. Israel is like a silly dove without heart. Thus saith the Lord: 'Turn again unto me, and I will betroth thee to me. I will love thee freely. I will be as the dew unto Israel; he shall grow as the lily and cast forth his roots as Lebanon.' "

For years Hosea spake thus, threatening, comforting, promising, for he had no logic of reasoning like the keenminded herdsman, Amos. He had only the depths of feeling of a tenderly loving heart. He chided sternly and passionately, and quickly stopped to comfort; for always he longed to comfort, but no one stopped to listen. He had no wife, no disciple, no human soul to help him. He stood apart from rulers and had no weight with princes. The people called him a fool and said that he was mad.

And in those days, Hosea came upon Gomer, his wife, exposed for sale as a slave in the public market place, deserted by all her lovers. And Hosea bought Gomer to him for fifteen pieces of silver, and an homer and an half of barley; and he took her back to his home and made her again his wife. And he knew that God was as ready to save His erring people.

But when Jeroboam died, Hosea saw war and bloodshed make sad the hearts of Israel; for Shal'lum slew Jeroboam's son and reigned a month in Samaria, and Men'a-hem slew Shallum, warring in barbarous fashion. And Pe'kah slew Menahem's son, and one, Hoshea, slew Pekah, making the seventh line of kings to sit on the throne of Israel, while on the throne of Judah sat only the line of David.

Troubled, grievous times were the days of the prophet, Hosea. He lived his life unheeded, with weight in no man's ears, but this great truth he added to the knowledge already gained concerning the nature of God—that God is not only just, but loving, forgiving, redeeming.

Little figurines discovered in Gezer and showing elaborate head-dresses, such as those which caused Isaiah to complain in the gorgeous days of the Kings Uzziah, Jotham, and Ahaz of Judah.   The woman to the left has a Phrygian cap.   The other figure has a braided cloak with sleeves, and a cap like a tam-o-shanter with six ribbons streaming behind.   The face appears to be tattooed on chin and lip as is common with women in Palestine today.

Isaiah, the Statesman of Judah
(760-701 B.C.)

Now when Jeroboam II reigned long and prosperously in Israel, King Uzziah was reigning long and prosperously in Judah. For sixty years before his time, Judah had had no sea-port; for Edom had revolted and taken with her Elath, Judah's only port of ships. Then a certain King Amaziah smote the Children of Edom and won back the port of Elath; and King Uzziah, his son, builded the city up till there rode once more in its harbor fleets of galleys with oars and many a gallant ship.

With a port again on the ocean, there came through the gates of Jerusalem great caravans of trade, bound for the world mart of Tyre on the Mediterranean Sea. And Jerusalem, so long shut up, became a door of the nations, the opened gates of the people. And her grandees turned to trade and made themselves fat with riches.

And Uzziah had an host of fighting men that made war with mighty power. And he built towers in Jerusalem, at the Corner Gate and the Valley Gate. And, great in peace as in war, he builded towers in the desert and digged many

Isaiah on the streets of Jerusalem, the city which he so loved. He sees the haughty women in all their overdone finery, and people crowding about the wizards who ply their trades. The wizard in the picture is divining the future from the clay model of a sheep's liver. He comes from Babylon, mistress of witch craft. See page 34.

wells, for he loved husbandry and had vinedressers on the mountains, and cattle in the plains. And his fame spread far abroad.

Now, in those days there was born of the upper class in Jerusalem, a boy named I-sa'iah. The lad admired the king and with all the strength of his fervent heart, he loved his native city, rising high and white, queenly on her hills, with mountains round about. He rambled through all Jerusalem, builded compactly together. He knew the Mak'tesh, where the merchants swarmed, the Baker's Street, smelling of freshly baked bread; the Fish Gate, the Horse Gate, the Valley Gate; the pools, the gardens, the narrow streets; and when he went up to the House of the Lord, he went with joy and gladness as one that pipes on a flute.

But the sudden growth of trade, the riches so newly won by a people long used to simple life, to farming and herding sheep, wrought grievous trouble in Judah; for a few grew very rich and gathered large estates, the judges took bribes of the rich, the prophets spake as they were hired, the princes lived at ease with feasting and drunken mirth, the people still worshiped at high places in the old evil Canaanite fashion, and they went to the temple of God as by rote, for their hearts were far from God.

Isaiah saw wizards plying their trade in streets and public places, and the silly folk crowding about them, seeking advice open-mouthed, and pleasantly thrilled with awe while the wizards peeped and muttered, pretending to call up shades of the dead by making their voices come out of the ground and whisper out of the dust. He met the women of Jerusalem, haughty, with stretched-forth necks, rolling wanton eyes, mincing as they walked, and making a tinkling sound, by means of anklets on their feet. He saw them decked out in moonshaped charms, with pendants and bracelets and rings, with earrings and nose-jewels and festival robes; with turbans and veils and shawls. And it was borne in on him slowly that his people were all perverted, headed for destruction. He had been a child when Amos appeared at Bethel, a boy when Hosea began to preach, but the words of both those prophets burned deep within his soul.

And signs of disaster came. Uzziah was stricken with leprosy as he stood within the temple, impatiently burning incense which was the right of the priest. And he was hurried away and dwelt in a separate house until the day of his death, and Jo'tham, his son, was regent in his stead.

And in the year that Uzziah died, Isaiah saw distinctly a new truth concerning God. He saw that God was not just alone, as Amos had seen so clearly, not loving alone, as Hosea had seen, but glorious and holy, possessing every excellence that may call forth adoration, with no taint of human frailty. He was not superior to other gods, He was truly the only God, the Holy *One* of Israel. And Isaiah saw in a vision clear to his inward eye, all the glory of God, as it were in the form of a man, sitting upon a throne, with seraphim singing above:

Holy, Holy, Holy, is the Lord of Hosts;
The whole earth is full of His glory.

And the foundations of the temple shook, and the house was filled with smoke. And when he beheld that glory, Isaiah's heart was smitten; for he saw how unlike God were he and his erring people. And he cried:

"Woe is me; for I am a man of unclean lips, and I dwell in the midst of a people of unclean lips."

Then in his vision he saw one among the seraphim take a live coal from the altar and lay it upon his mouth; the flaming brightness of fire burning up all impurity, cleansing him of his sin. And thereafter he heard the voice of the Lord, saying: "Whom shall I send to this people?"

And Isaiah made answer at once: "Here am I; send me!"

And the Lord said: "Go and tell my people: 'Ye hear, but understand not. Ye see, indeed, but perceive not.' "

And Isaiah said: "How long will the people be thus blind?"

And the Lord said: "Till the cities be wasted and the land be utterly desolate. Nevertheless a tenth shall be saved to carry on the holy seed, the real knowledge of God."

And Isaiah called his first-born son She'ar-ja'shub, meaning "A-remnant-shall-be-saved." And he went forth and pleaded tenderly, yet sternly with his people: "O house of Jacob, come ye, let us walk in the light of the Lord."

Now Jotham, the strong king, died, and there came to the throne of Judah, A'haz, his son, a petulant youth, ruled by his household of women; he who burned incense on high places and under every green tree, and had a court more wild, more arrogant and drunken, than any that went before.

Then Re'zin, King of Syria, and Pekah, King of Israel, made a league against Judah, for Syria meant to take to herself the valuable port of Elath, and they plotted to make another king in place of the line of David that had reigned so long in Judah. And the allies took towns in Judah and carried captives away; and they came to the gates of Jerusalem. And the

Tiglath Pileser III, of Assyria. He mentions in his inscriptions Men'a-hem, Pekah and Hoshea, kings of Israel; Ahaz of Judah, and Rezin of Damascus. (See page 68.)

people fell into a panic. The heart of the king and the hearts of his people shook as the trees of the wood, when their leaves are moved by the wind. And Ahaz saw no means of escape save to send unto Tig'lath-Pi-le'ser, the warrior king of Assyria, and beg for the help of his hosts.

Isaiah alone kept his head. He saw that to call in Assyria, would be for his people to bend their necks to the yoke of the world's worst tyrant; whereas, if they only waited, Assyria would of her own accord rise up and destroy their foe. And he took his small son called A-remnant-shall-be-saved, and appeared before Ahaz in the highway of the fuller's field. And he said: "Fear not, for Rezin, king of Syria, and Pekah, king of Israel, are smoking stumps of firebrands, ready to go out."

But Ahaz would not hearken nor turn his heart to God. Indeed, in the time of trouble he trespassed further and said: "The gods of Rezin help him; therefore will I sacrifice to them that they may help me!"

And he sacrificed unto the gods of Damascus.

Isaiah posts in a public place the placard foretelling that Israel and Syria would fall speedy prey before Assyria.

Then Isaiah wrote in large letters upon a great placard and said: "Hurried prey—speedy spoil" (Ma'her-shal'al-hash'baz), and he put it up in a public place that all who passed might read. Israel would fall hurried prey; Syria would fall speedy spoil before the wolf Assyria. And he named his second son Hurried-prey-Speedy-spoil, to be for a sign to the people.

But still they would not hearken, for Ahaz took the silver and gold from the House of the Lord and sent it to Tiglath-Pileser, saying: "I am thy servant. Come up and save me."

And the King of Assyria took Damascus and carried the people of it away captive and slew Rezin. And he punished Israel, but left Pekah on the throne. And with Syria conquered, the very last barrier was broken down that had kept Assyria from Judah. Judah, herself, had opened the door to let Assyria in. And Ahaz went to Damascus, to kiss the ground before Tiglath-Pileser; and in that terrible day, he who had sold Judah's liberties, could think of naught more important than a fine new fashion in altars which he beheld in Damascus and of which he sent a pattern home that one might be built in Jerusalem.

And Isaiah said in great sadness: "My people have gone into captivity because they have no knowledge. The Lord Jehovah said: 'By returning and rest ye shall be saved. In quietness and confidence shall be your strength;' and ye would not."

And he went and dwelt apart with his wife, and his sons,

A terra cotta altar of incense of the time of Ahaz, the eighth century, B.C., found at Ta'a-nach in Palestine, and belonging to a private house.

It was some such altar as this perhaps that so deeply interested Ahaz. The box has no bottom. A fire was lit on the ground and the box placed over it.

The altar consists of a pile of figures. Manheaded figures with wings, wearing short caps with tassels, and intended to represent cherubs, stand on the backs of lions. Below the top of the altar is a carved handle. The work is crude but interesting, neither Egyptian nor Assyrian, but apparently true Hebrew.

and disciples which he had gathered; but he spake no more for many years to the people or the King. Nevertheless, he dwelt ever more surely in thought, on the ideal state to come—when Judah should have suffered enough to recognize her faults and cast them from her forever; when the ransomed of the Lord should return and come to Zion with songs and everlasting joy upon their heads; when the eyes of the blind should be opened, the ears of the deaf unstopped; when the lame man should leap as an hart, and the tongue of the dumb, sing. His was a joyful spirit, calm, peace-loving, hopeful, full of confident trust in the goodness and joy of God. And he often dreamed of a saviour who should come to help his people; but he saw that saviour as a king of the line of David and Jesse, who should sit on the throne in Jerusalem, and rule in such absolute justice that all the nations of earth should come to this new Jerusalem for the joy of her lasting peace.

"Behold, a king shall reign in righteousness. And the Spirit of the Lord shall rest upon him, the spirit of wisdom and understanding, the spirit of counsel and might. And he shall not judge after the sight of his eyes, neither reprove after the hearing of his ears; but with righteousness shall he judge. And the Lord's House shall be established and all nations shall flow unto it. And they shall beat their swords into ploughshares and their spears into pruning hooks; nation shall not lift up sword against nation; neither shall they learn war any more. The wolf also shall dwell with the lamb, and the leopard shall lie down with the kid; and the calf and the young lion and the fatling together; and a little child shall lead them. They shall not hurt nor destroy in all my holy mountain; for the earth shall be full of the knowledge of the Lord as the waters cover the sea."

Thus did Isaiah dream.

Now Ahaz died in process of time and his son, Hez'e-ki'ah, reigned. And the new king kept the Passover and began to take away high places and do much good in the land; yet Hezekiah was weak, and he leaned for all his counsel on Sheb'na, his prime minister, and a powerful party for war.

Then Hoshea, King of Israel, made alliance with So, King of Egypt, and rebelled against Assyria in company with Philistia and other little nations; whereon, Hezekiah and Shebna likewise thought to rebel. But Isaiah came forth at last from his many long years of retirement to cry against such a step:

"Woe to them that go down to Egypt for help and trust in chariots because they are many; and in horsemen because they are strong; but they look not unto the Holy One of Israel, neither seek the Lord! Now the Egyptians are men and not God, and their horses flesh and not spirit, and they all shall fail together. The Lord shall defend Jerusalem. Turn ye unto Him!"

And there rose one Mi'cah, the Mo'res-thite, a poor man of the people, dwelling in a village of Judah, near the Philistine lowlands, which was the scene of war; and he spake in the villages, while Isaiah spake in the city. And Micah beheld in the storm ready to burst on Judah, Jehovah going forth in righteous indignation to visit the sins of the land. And he cried:

"Behold, the Lord cometh forth and for the transgressions of Jacob, the mountains shall be molten under him; the valleys shall be cleft!"

"Will the Lord be pleased with thousands of rams or with ten thousand rivers of oil? He hath showed thee, O man, what is good; and what doth the Lord require of thee but to do justly, to love mercy and to walk humbly with thy God?"

Micah preaches to the common people. Micah was a poor man of the countryside, talking to farmers and villagers while Isaiah spoke in Jerusalem, a city man, nobly born, talking to men of the city; but both bore much the same message,—Judah knows what is good; let her do it or she will fall.

Assyrians besieging a city, from a bas-relief found at Nimrud and now in the British Museum. At the right is the King protected by his shield bearer. Before the King is a movable tower with a battering ram. Enemy soldiers try to grapple the ram with chains or set it afire. At the left Assyrians are digging down the city wall with iron crow-bars. Residents of the city shoot from the walls, women standing by the men to urge them on in battle.

Then came Shalmaneser, King of Assyria, and besieged Samaria and took it and carried away the ten tribes of Israel and scattered them among all nations till they lived no more as a race but lost all knowledge of God and walked in the way of the heathen. Henceforth they were ever called

Assyrians carrying women and children captive from a town in Asia. A bas-relief found at Nimrud and now in the British Museum. This picture might well represent the women and children of Samaria being carried away from the city. From a side-gate come ox-carts carrying the captives to exile. At the right a shepherd drives off booty,—flocks of sheep, goats and cattle. Two scribes are reporting to a higher Assyrian official the amount of the spoil they have taken. At the left a battering ram stands, idle after the battle.

the ten lost tribes of Israel. And Shalmaneser filled all the land of Israel with people of foreign races who strove with lions and other wild beasts to possess the desolate ruins. So ended the northern kingdom never again to revive.

Nevertheless, in secret, Judah still said in her heart: "Let us make alliance with Egypt!"

Therefore Isaiah came forth again to show a striking sign. He walked abroad naked and barefoot, saying, "So shall the King of Assyria lead the Egyptians captive, naked and barefoot to their shame. And if they fare so, to whom we flee for help, how can we escape?"

For three years Isaiah walked naked, silently protesting. But when Sargon, King of Assyria, died, and his son, Sennach'e-rib, reigned, one Me-ro'dach Bal'a-dan, a turbulent prince of Babylon, came up out of his marshes and rebelled against Sennacherib, sending presents and a letter unto King Hezekiah to ask concerning his health, but with the

Isaiah walks naked and barefoot protesting alliance with Egypt. Isaiah protested with silence or with the most fervid eloquence. When he spoke he often fell into the measured cadence of poetry, for he had the mind of a poet. The life and words of Isaiah are given in the Book of Isaiah, Chapters 1 to 40. After Chapter 40 the words of a second prophet called the Unknown Comforter, have been added to this book. (See page 265.)

Merodach Baladan, the prince of Babylon who rebelled against Sennacherib. From an Assyrian carving. (See page 72.)

secret intent of getting King Hezekiah to join him in his revolt. And Hezekiah made much display to receive the men of Babylon, for he meant in his heart to join them. But Isaiah rebuked him sternly.

"There is only one way," he cried, "whereby ye may find peace! The work of righteousness shall be peace, and the effect of righteousness quietness and assurance forever."

Therefore, for fear of Isaiah, Shebna worked in secret, sending a camel-train privately bearing rich treasures to Egypt and soon it was openly known that Judah had rebelled.

Then came Sen-nach'er-ib (in 701 B.C.) and took the proud city of Tyre, the mart of the nations, whose merchants were princes. He subdued the Philistine cities; and when he had thrown his army to shut off Judah from Egypt, he turned his forces inland, taking the cities of Judah, and marching ever nearer, nearer the City of David. "All her land," he boasted in graven records of stone, "I swept like a mighty whirlwind; 34 great cities I ravaged; the smoke of their burning like a mighty cloud obscured the face of heaven."

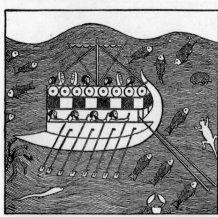

The Kings of Tyre and Sidon in a Phoenician war galley flee before Sennacherib.

On the upper deck of the galley are the royal passengers shielded by awnings attached to the mast. Below on each side are eight oarsmen, four above and four below. Shields and black and white squares decorate the sides of the ship and the prow is a prong made to ram an enemy's vessel. From an Assyrian stone carving. (See page 72.)

Panic arose in Jerusalem. The people set to work with feverish haste on the walls, tearing down houses to furnish bricks to fill in the yawning breaches. And Hezekiah sealed up the mouth of the spring of Gi'hon that opened outside the city and made a tunnel to carry the water seventeen hundred feet inside the city walls. Yet no real hope was felt, no calm and confident courage.

Workmen in Hezekiah's tunnel. From a photograph of the tunnel as it is today.

Here was found the Si-lo'am inscription telling how the workmen beginning at both ends met in the center of the tunnel. The tunnel was 1700 feet long with a diameter of from two to eleven feet, a wonderful piece of engineering, to have been made with neither compass nor level.

The inscription says: "This was the manner of the piercing through. While yet (the diggers were lifting up) the pick, each towards his fellow, and while yet there were three cubits to be cut (through, each heard) the voice of one calling to his fellow, for there was a crack (?) in the rock on the south. And on the day of the piercing through, the diggers struck pick against pick, one over against the other, and there flowed the water from the source of the pool, 1,200 cubits."

The people swarmed to the temple and offered rich sacrifices, but with no thought of cleansing their hearts or changing their evil ways. They still hoped to win Jehovah by sacrifices and offerings. And Isaiah cried with great force, "Bring no more vain oblations! Wash you, make you clean!"

Nearer, ever nearer, drew the dread King of Assyria, till Hezekiah, in terror, sent him great tribute of treasures and made submission to him. Then the men of Judah rose, hurled Shebna from his post, and with him the party for war; and they put in Shebna's place, Isaiah's friend, E-li'a-kim.

Thus Isaiah became at last adviser to Hezekiah, and while Sennacherib left them in peace, they worked many great reforms; for they took away the high places and said unto the people, "Ye shall worship at one altar only, the altar of the Lord." And they cleansed the land of her idols and turned the people about to obey the law of the Lord.

The siege of Lachish, from the walls of Sennacherib's palace at Nineveh. Archers and spearmen behind their shields fight their way up the hill. In the right foreground are slingers, with heaps of stones at their feet. In the left center citizens surrendering come out of a side gate and three naked rebel leaders are shown impaled in stakes. From the walls men hurl burning torches down on the wooden battering rams, but Assyrians with dippers on long poles pour water in front of the rams. Scaling ladders are being knocked off the walls.

Matters went well in Jerusalem until Sennacherib learned that Tir-ha′kah, King of Egypt, was finally marching against him. These tidings reached his ears as he lay encamped before La′chish, and he felt he had greatly erred in leaving King Hezekiah upon the throne of Judah; so, he sent up against Jerusalem his captains and a great host.

But Jerusalem under Isaiah was now a different place. Purged of the worst of her sins, Jerusalem could not fall,— Isaiah was sure of that. The City of David must be preserved, to save the knowledge of God. As yet there were few sacred books, few spiritually minded men to teach a nation in exile. If Jerusalem had fallen then, if the people had then been parted from their temple and sacred places, knowledge of God would have died, as it did with the ten tribes of Israel. Isaiah knew she must stand. And his confidence shed assurance throughout the troubled land.

Peasants of Judah coming before Sennacherib at Lachish. The King sits on a great throne while his officers present the prisoners, who fall to their knees before him. At the upper left come two women of Judah with a child. Behind the king is his tent. Below, the king's chariot waits and a servant with the royal umbrella.

Hezekiah said to his people: "Be not afraid nor dismayed for the King of Assyria, nor for all the multitude that is with him, for there be more with us than with him. With him is an arm of flesh; but with us is the Lord our God, to help us and to fight our battles."

And the people rested themselves on the words of Hezekiah.

And the Rab'sa-ris, Rab'sha-keh and Tartan, officers of the Hosts of Assyria, came up and showed themselves, standing before Jerusalem, and they cried aloud in the language of the Jews to frighten the men on the walls: "Egypt on whom you lean is naught but a broken reed that can only pierce your hand. Hezekiah hath said: 'Trust in the Lord your God,' but he hath broken your altars,—you have no God to help you. Submit to the King of Assyria!"

A heavy-armed Assyrian horseman and a war chariot with a driver and three soldiers (668-624 B.C.). The horses are beautifully modelled. Parts of a bas-relief found at Nineveh and now at the Louvre.

Then Eliakim came and said: "I pray thee speak in the Syrian tongue, for we can understand it. Talk not in the Jews' tongue in the ears of all the people!"

But the Rabshakeh only cried louder in the language of the Jews and said: "Hath the god of any nation delivered his land from the King of Assyria? How then shall the Lord, thy God, deliver Jerusalem from him?"

No word did the people answer him; for the king's commandment was: "Answer him not a word."

Nevertheless, in secret, King Hezekiah feared. And he rent his clothes and sent Eliakim with elders of the priests clad in sackcloth, unto Isaiah, saying: "Lift up thy prayer for the remnant."

And Isaiah wrote words of comfort unto King Hezekiah: "Be not afraid of what thou hast heard; for the King of Assyria shall return to his own land."

And Hezekiah went up to the House of the Lord and prayed: "Of a truth, Lord, the kings of Assyria have destroyed the nations and cast their gods into the fire, for they were no gods but the work of men's hands, carven of wood and stone.

"Now, therefore, O Lord our God, I beseech thee, save us out of his hand that all the kingdoms of earth may know thou art the Lord God, even thou only."

And when the people rose up early in the morning, lo, the army of Assyria had vanished from the plain. Its camp lay deserted and desolate, and none knows why to this day. Mayhap Sennacherib called it back in haste

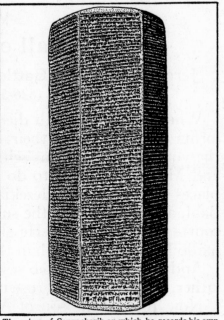

The prism of Sennacherib on which he records his own boastful story of his doings in Palestine, now in the Oriental Institute, University of Chicago. (Page 72.)

to meet the Egyptians. Mayhap some plague destroyed it. But whatever the reason, it vanished.

Isaiah's words were proved true; Jerusalem was saved, and the people cried aloud:

'God is our refuge and strength,
A very present help in trouble."

And Isaiah and Hezekiah wrought many reforms in Judah. They took away the high places in all the towns and villages and made Jerusalem alone one central place of worship, one altar to one God. And Isaiah saw his teachings succeed, to some extent at least. He saw a people, purer, returned to their one God, worshipping with the heart, not merely with outward form, resting in the quiet and confidence he had promised, and singing his song of glory: "Holy, Holy, Holy is the Lord of Hosts."

VIII

The Fall of Jerusalem

Jeremiah and His Battle with the False Prophets
(626-586 B.C.)

When King Hezekiah died, they who hated Isaiah's reforms and longed for their idols again, gained control of the young King Ma-nas'seh, a boy only twelve years old; and Manasseh began to do evil, for he built up the high places destroyed by Hezekiah, and reared up altars for Baal, and worshipped the sun, moon and stars in the very courts of the temple. He shed much innocent blood and made Judah do worse than the heathen.

And Amon, Manasseh's son, walked in the ways of his father, till his servants rose up and slew him.

Now Josiah, the son of Amon, was likewise a boy but eight years old when he began to reign. But Josiah did that which was right and sought after the God of David.

And in his twentieth year Josiah began to purge Judah from the high places and the sacred poles and the graven images.

Two priests, a high priest perhaps, and a common priest holding up an animal for sacrifice. Note the long robes, the tall caps and the beard on the man at the right. (A seal from Gezer.)

But his people had a rebellious heart; they refused to receive correction; they made their faces harder than a rock, for they still burned incense on the roofs unto the sun and moon and all the host of heaven. They still caused their children to pass through the fire unto Moloch and worshipped idols on every high hill and under every green tree. The rich still oppressed the poor; and they said in their stubborn hearts: "The Lord can do no good, neither can He do evil!"

The vase above was found in a Scythian tomb at Kul Oba. It shows these barbarians in thick double-breasted coats edged with fur, and held in by a belt. They wear trousers tucked into soft leather boots tied around the ankle and are the first people known to wear trousers instead of skirts or robes. On their heads are high pointed hoods that come close around the neck. To the left a Scythian strings his short Tartar bow. To the right, one Scythian pulls another's tooth. In the middle is the clay model of a covered Scythian ox-cart found on the bank of the Sajur.

Then, behold, there came out of the north a horde of wild barbarians, Scythians from the Russian steppes, bearing their women and children in clumsy covered wagons.

Robbing, pillaging, plundering, they threatened to pour into Judah and overwhelm the land.

From 800 to 600 B.C., these wild Scythians dwelt on the treeless plains of South Russia; but about 600 B.C., they poured down into Asia. Armenians and Assyrians were unable to resist them. They advanced to the borders of Egypt, striking terror to all the land; but they founded no great kingdom. They vanished at last by melting into other civilizations. The figures in this picture are taken from the models above.

The prophet Zephaniah, a royal Prince of Judah, warning Jerusalem in Jeremiah's youth. Zephaniah appears in pictures with a lamp, because he said God would search with a lamp to bring evil to light and destroy it.

And Zeph-a-ni'ah, the Prince, thundered forth vivid warnings: "The day of the Lord is near! It is near and hasteth greatly. That day is a day of wrath, of wasteness and desolation. 'At that time,' saith the Lord, 'I will search Jerusalem with a lamp and punish them that do evil!' Seek the Lord, all ye meek —seek righteousness! Seek meekness! The just Lord is here to save thee. He will joy over thee with singing!'"

Yet even with wild barbarians swarming up to their gates, the people refused to hearken.

And in those days there dwelt of a family of priests in An'a-thoth, a youth named Jeremiah. And Jeremiah heard in his soul the voice of the Lord as an holy urge, saying: "I have ordained thee a prophet unto the nations."

Nevertheless, Jeremiah was young; he was shy and humble of spirit, and he said, "Lord, God, behold! I cannot speak; for I am no more than a child."

But the Lord said unto him: "Say not I am a child; for thou shalt go to all that I shall send thee, and whatsoever I command thee, thou shalt speak. Be not afraid of their faces; for I am with thee to deliver thee. Gird up thy loins, and go."

And the youth arose and left the fields of his fathers, the stone quarries and olive groves of the ancient town of Anathoth, and he went an hours' journey southward till he saw before him Jerusalem, beautiful for situation, the joy of the whole earth, the city of the great king.

The youth Jeremiah beholding in the streets of Jerusalem the joy and innocent mirth which he so loved.

And as he entered the gates, he heard the voice of mirth and the voice of gladness, the voice of the bridegroom and the voice of the bride; he beheld the children at play, the virgin rejoicing in the dance; and he yearned to preserve that joy that it might not be turned into mourning.

His heart made a noise within him. He could not hold his peace, lest those people, now so merry, should flee from the noise of horsemen, and go into thickets for safety and climb up upon the rocks.

And he cried in the ears of Jerusalem, saying:

"Behold, a people cometh from the north country! They lay hold on bow and spear! They are cruel and have no mercy! Their voice roareth like the sea, and they ride upon horses!

"O Jerusalem, wash thine heart from wickedness that thou mayest be saved. How long shall thy vain thoughts lodge in thee? Hast thou not procured this trouble unto thyself in that thou hast forsaken the Lord thy God when He led thee by the way? Wherefore trimmest thou thy way to seek love? Wilt thou not from this time cry unto God: 'My father, thou art the guide of my youth'? Truly in the Lord our God is the salvation of Israel!"

But the Scythians took their course unto Egypt by way of the sea-coast and came not up into Judah. And there was joy and thanksgiving in all the cities of Judah.

Then Josiah ordered that the temple should be repaired; and while workmen wrought in the house, Hil-ki'ah, the High Priest, found a book of the law, (the same is Deu'ter-on'o-my,) hidden beneath the floor. And Sha'phan, the Scribe, took the book and thus did he read before the King:

"Hear, O Israel, the Lord our God is one Lord, and thou shalt love the Lord thy God with all thine heart and with all thy soul and with all thy might. Ye shall utterly destroy all the places wherein the nations which ye shall possess served their gods, upon the high mountains and upon the hills and under every green tree."

And when the King had heard the words of the book, he rent his clothes, so far were his erring people from keeping such a law. And he went up unto the temple and stood by a pillar of the porch and read the words of the book in the ears of all the people. And the hearts of the people were smitten, and they made a covenant there to walk in the law of the Lord and do the words of the book.

And Josiah put down the idolatrous priests who burned incense unto Baal, to the sun, the moon, the stars and all the host of heaven. And he brake down the houses where the women wove hangings for the sacred pole.

A winged creature with a scimitar slaying an animal. At the left, a flaming sun, at the right a crescent moon. These figures show the confused worship of the time. From a seal of the period found at Gezer.

And he defiled Tophet, which is in the Valley of the Children of Hin'nom, that no man might make his son or his daughter to pass through the fire to Moloch. And he took away the horses that the kings of Judah had given to the sun at the entering in of the

The Valley of Hinnom outside Jerusalem, where the people made their children to pass through the fire to Moloch.

house of the Lord, and burned the chariots of the sun with fire.

Moreover, the workers with familiar spirits and the wizards and the images in all the land of Judah did Josiah put away that he might perform all the words of the book.

And Jeremiah, the youth, journeyed through Judah, saying: "Hear ye the words of this covenant and do them."

Then Josiah commanded the people to keep a Passover unto the Lord. And there was no Passover like that kept in Israel from the days of Samuel, the prophet.

Now after this, King Josiah reigned for fifteen years. But Ne'cho, king of Egypt, had heard that the King of Assyria was hard pressed in his land. The Scythians had smitten him. The Medes and the Babylonians pressed upon his sides. And Pharaoh Necho said: "Now shall I take from Assyria, Syria and Judah that once paid tribute to Egypt!"

And he went up toward the Euphrates, to fight with the King of Assyria, and he took his way through Judah.

Then Josiah went out against him, and Necho sent ambassadors unto Josiah, saying: "What have I to do with thee, thou King of Judah? I came not against thee this day but against the house of Assyria, wherewith I have war."

But Josiah went forth, notwithstanding. And the archers shot Josiah; and the young King said to his servants: "Have me away; for I am sore wounded."

His servants therefore took him in his chariot unto Jerusalem, and he died. And all Judah and Jerusalem, the singing men and the singing women mourned for Josiah. And Jeremiah lamented; for like unto Josiah was there no king before that turned to the Lord with all his heart and with all his soul and with all his might.

And Necho went on his way unto the river Euphrates, but the King of Assyria, sore beset, came not down against him. Therefore Necho, without a battle, declared himself lord over Judah. In three months time he came back and took Je-ho'a-haz, son of Josiah, who sat on the throne of Judah, and bore him a captive to Egypt, and he made Josiah's second son, Je-hoi'a-kim, king in his stead and he put the land to a tribute.

Semitic captives laboring in Nineveh. Such a captive was Nahum, author of the Book of Nahum. From Assyrian carvings.

Then evil days came on Judah; for the people cried aloud in passionate impatience: "We did right and still we suffer. Josiah reigned in justice and still Josiah perished." And they would wait no longer to see the day of good; but flung aside faith in God, and turned again to their idols as in the days of Manasseh. The children gathered wood, the fathers kindled the fire, and the

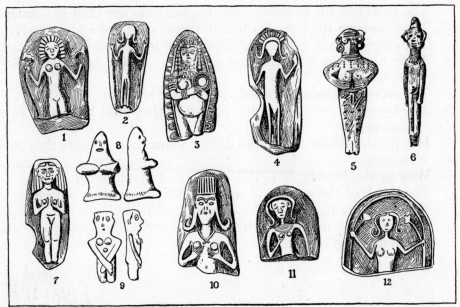

The Egyptian Queen of Heaven Ha'thor, against whose worship Jeremiah so bitterly complained, was quite generally confused with Ashtoreth, Ishtar or Astarte, the earth-mother of the Chaldeans. Scores of Hathor-Astoreth placques have been found in Gezer and elsewhere. Usually these figures are offering their breasts to the world, in token that the goddess is the source of material sustenance and growth. (1) has a curly wig and carries lotus lilies; (2) is a crude plaque of Jeremiah's own time; (3) has a veil, armlets and a tambourine; (4) has hair sticking up like a nimbus; (5) is an Ishtar figure from Ashur in Assyria; (6) is a horned Astarte; (7) has the hair covered with a veil; (8) and (9) are crude rounded figures of Jeremiah's time; (10) has a cylindrical crown made of feathers; (11) has the typical "S" shaped Hathor wig, and a necklace of three strands; and (12) has the "S" shaped wig and lotus lilies.

women kneaded their dough to make cakes to the Queen of Heaven. On the rooftops, they offered incense to Baal; they poured out drink-offerings unto other gods. And Jeremiah's days of joyous work were done. "Ye have forsaken the Lord," he cried, "the fountain of living waters!"

And within two full years came news that Nineveh was besieged. The age-long oppressor of Judah, the lion that stalked in darkness devouring smaller nations, was ripe at last for destruction. Cy-ax'a-res, King of the Medes, and Na-bo-po-las'sar of Babylon, stood at the gates of Nineveh, long so unassailable with her twelve hundred mighty towers and her wall an hundred feet high. And Na'hum, an exile of Israel, dwelling in far Assyria, wrote home with fiery joy:

The shield of his heroes is red, his warriors are clad in scarlet;
They prepare the chariots today, the chariot horses are eager.
The chariots rage in the fields; they rush to and fro in the plazas;
Their appearance is like that of torches, they dart about like
  the lightnings.
The river sluices are opened, the palace walls are crumbling;
The Queen is stripped of her clothing; they lead her away as a
  captive;
Her handmaidens moan like doves; upon their breasts they are
  beating.
Woe to the bloody city, full of lies and of plunder;
The crack of the whip and the thunder of rumbling wheels;
The prancing horse and the bounding chariot;
The horsemen mounting, the flash of sword, the gleam of spear,
  and an heap of slain!

Nahum, the exiled Jew, beholds the fall of Nineveh.   Medes and Chaldeans storm the city.   (See page 321.)

Nineveh as it is today, no more than an heap in the desert.   The distant mound is Nineveh.   From a photograph.

So Nineveh fell, to be henceforth only an heap in the desert. Flocks lay down in the midst of her, wild beasts prowled through her ruins, cormorants and bitterns perched in her broken windows. And Nahum wrote again, thinking the fall of that one war-lord meant peace for all the world:

"Behold upon the mountains the feet of him
That bringeth good tidings and publisheth peace!"

And all the false prophets of Judah, ever speaking that which the people wished to hear, but never daring to state the plain unpopular truth, said: "Now your troubles are over. No evil shall come upon you!"

But the heart of Jeremiah wept in secret places and his eyes ran down with tears; for he saw as none before him had ever seen so clearly, that real salvation from evil was wholly an inner matter, correction of heart and thought, no superficial question of outward circumstance. He looked for no ease for his people, while their hearts were still so evil. And then began his long struggle, with those false prophets of the guilds who prophesied peace for hire. And he cried:

"Thus saith the Lord: 'They have healed the hurt of the daughter of my people slightly, saying: Peace! Peace! when there is no peace. Hear, O earth, I will bring evil upon this people, even the fruit of their thoughts!' "

And he knew full well that either Egypt or Babylon would tread in Assyria's footsteps as tyrant over Judah, from whom there was no escape, save by the strength and courage of hearts so clean and faithful they dared to trust in God. And he stood forth boldly in the court of the temple and said: "If ye will not walk in the law of the Lord, this city shall be desolate, a curse unto all the earth!"

And the people were full of rage and they crowded about him, saying, "Thou shalt surely die!"

But while the people debated, A-hi'kam, son of Shaphan, who had read the book of the law in the ears of King Josiah, hastened to lead Jeremiah secretly out of the temple.

And Jeremiah cried, "O that I had in the wilderness a lodging place for wayfaring men, that I might go from my people."

And he went unto Anathoth to his brethren and the house of his father, to refresh himself in a land of peace wherein he trusted. But he was like a lamb or an ox that is brought to the slaughter; for even his brethren dealt treacherously. They spake fair words to his face, but they called a multitude after him, seeking his life and saying: "Speak no more evil prophecies lest thou die by our hand!"

Jeremiah driven by his own family from Anathoth. Background from a photograph of the village of Anathoth.

And Jeremiah returned unto Jerusalem, longing to give forth love, but everywhere meeting with hatred, loving the voice of joy, but forced to preach destruction, loving Judah with all his heart, but ever accounted a traitor.

And he sat alone in the city. He took no wife, neither had he sons nor daughters in the land. Not for him were the joy of the bride adorned with her ornaments, the light of the lamp at eventide, the laughter of little children. Yea, he sat alone like a pelican of the wilderness, a sparrow alone on the housetop. And he cried:

"Woe is me, my mother, that thou hast borne me a man of strife to all the earth, for every one doth curse me!"

Now it came to pass in the fourth year of Jehoiakim that Neb-u-chad-nez'zar, King of Babylon, went out against Pharaoh Necho unto Carchemish by the river Euphrates. The horsemen came up; the chariots raged! But the mighty men of Egypt were beaten and fled apace and Nebuchadnezzar stood forth, new war-lord of the earth.

Then was there rejoicing in Judah because their foe, Necho, had fallen, but Jeremiah said: "Nebuchadnezzar will come and destroy this land with fire."

And the people took Jeremiah and cast him into prison, and ever more clearly he saw that the hearts of his people had grown so hard with pride and self-satisfaction, that only utter destruction, the ruin of Jerusalem and carrying the people captive away to a foreign land, would waken them up to think, to acknowledge their faults and forsake them.

And he called Ba'ruch, his friend, and bade him write down on a roll, all the words he had spoken.

And he said: "Go and read from this roll in the ears of all the people."

And Baruch went to the temple, to the chamber of Sha-phan, the Scribe, and he read: "The King of Babylon shall certainly come and destroy this land with fire!"

Jehoiakim in a rage destroys Jeremiah's scroll as he sits in his winterhouse with his princes. The lamp is copied from one found at Gezer. The bird is of clay, but the feathers are real feathers inserted in holes at the side.

And one went unto the King's house where the princes were sitting, and told them the words of Ba'ruch. And the princes sent to Baruch, saying: "Come with thy roll unto us."

So Baruch came and read the book; and the princes were afraid and said: "We will tell the king these words, but hide, thou and Jeremiah, that no man know where ye be."

And Je-hu'di read the words of the roll in the ears of the King. Now the King sat in the winter-house in the ninth month, and there was a fire on the hearth before him. And he snatched the roll from Jehudi and slashed it with a pen-knife and cast it into the fire till the roll was all consumed.

And he sent his servants to seize Baruch and Jeremiah; but they were hidden in safety.

And Jeremiah took another roll and Baruch wrote therein all the unpopular prophecies which Jehoiakim had destroyed.

Now Nebuchadnezzar came, as Jeremiah had foretold; Jehoiakim became his servant and paid him tribute three years. Then Jehoiakim rebelled and all the people with him.

And Jeremiah went down to the potter's house, and behold the potter wrought a work on the wheel. And the vessel that he made of clay was marred in his hand; so he made it again, another vessel as seemed good to the potter to make it. And Jeremiah took a vessel and went to the Valley of Hin'nom where the people caused their children to pass through the fire unto Moloch. And he cried:

"Thus saith the Lord: Behold as clay is in the potter's hand, so are ye in mine hand, O house of Israel. Because ye have forsaken me, and filled this valley with blood, I will make this city desolate. Even so will I break this people as one breaketh a potter's vessel that can never be made whole!"

And he hurled the vessel down to the ground and brake it before them all.

Then he went from the Valley of Hinnom to the court of the temple and said: "Thus saith the Lord: 'Behold, I will bring on this city all the evil that I have pronounced against it!'"

Jeremiah watches the potter make a pot on his wheel. The vessels are copied exactly from pots found at Gezer. Elaborate, geometric designs now have largely replaced the quaint animals of the next earlier period.

Pashur, the high priest puts Jeremiah in the stocks.

And Pash'ur, the High Priest, hearing his words, smote him in a rage and put him in the stocks within the High Gate of Benjamin. And the heart of Jeremiah was bitter and he cried: "Cursed be the day wherein I was born! I am in derision daily. Everyone mocketh me! I will not make mention of the Lord, nor speak any more in His name!"

But the words of the Lord were fire in his heart and he could not forbear. And on the morrow when Pashur came and brought him forth from the stocks, he cried aloud as beforetime: "Thus saith the Lord: 'Judah shall fall to Babylon!' Thou Pashur, shalt die a captive, thou and all thy friends."

And Nebuchadnezzar came and bound Jehoiakim in fetters to take him to Babylon, and he made his son, Jehoi'a-chin, king in his stead. But in three months' time he returned and laid siege to Jerusalem, and Jehoiachin went out and gave himself up to the King of Babylon, and with him went his mother, the Queen, with all the palace officials.

And Nebuchadnezzar carried away captive unto Babylon, all the men of valor, the princes and the craftsmen, the carpenters and smiths, and E-ze'ki-el, the priest, the friend of Jeremiah; even ten thousand captives, with all the vessels and treasures of the temple and the palace.

And Jeremiah was no more young when he saw that long train of captives, the flower of the land he loved, depart to go unto Babylon. For twenty-nine years had he labored in vain to turn Judah back from her folly.

And many there were in those days who cried with a very great bitterness: "Why is this evil come on us? Why does an evil race conquer?"

And Ha-bak'kuk stood forth to question and challenge an honest answer. And waiting as on a watch tower, he heard the answer that came, and he said: "I will write it on tablets plainly that he may run that readeth it." And thus did Habakkuk write:

Habbakuk puts up his message on a placard that even those who run by may read it.

"The vision of final good is yet for the time to come; but at the end it shall speak and not lie. Though it tarry, wait for it, because it will surely come; for it is not the will of the Lord that the people should labor in the fire. The earth shall be filled with the knowledge of the glory of the Lord as the waters cover the sea."

Now the King of Babylon made Zed-e-ki'ah, third son of Josiah, king over Judah. And Zedekiah paid Nebuchadnezzar tribute for nine years, but he hearkened not unto Jeremiah nor humbled himself before him.

And at the end of nine years, Pharaoh Hoph'ra came to the throne of Egypt in place of his father, Necho, and he began anew to stir up agitation among the little nations that they should rebel against Babylon. And Moab and Ammon sent messengers urging rebellion, to Judah. And Zedekiah rebelled, seeking horses and warriors of Egypt, while all the professional prophets promised a triumph to Judah.

And Jeremiah cried: "Mine heart within me is broken because of the prophets. The folly of trusting in Egypt!"

Jeremiah, as usual with the prophets, teaches the people by giving a dramatic sign. He comes forth wearing an ox yoke. Hananiah seizes the yoke to break it. Jeremiah's great struggle is now with the guild of prophets, public teachers of religion who from Elijah's day dwelt together in schools wearing a camel's hair garment girt with a leather belt. At first they honestly sought to guide the people wisely in obedience to the law of God, but in the time of Amos they were growing worldly-minded so the true prophets avoided them, and now in Jeremiah's time they were little better than hired agitators swaying the moods of the people according as they were paid (page 191).

And he put on his neck an ox yoke of wood and stood in the court of the temple, crying: "Bring your necks under the yoke of the King of Babylon and live. Hearken not to the words of the prophets that say unto you: Rebel; 'for I have not sent them,' saith the Lord. They prophesy a lie!"

Then Han'a-ni'ah, a false prophet, cried: "Thus saith the Lord: 'I have broken the yoke of Babylon. Within two years will I bring home again all the captives of Judah.' "

But Jeremiah said: "Amen. When thy words come true, then shall it be known that the Lord hath truly sent thee!"

Whereupon Hananiah raged and brake the yoke in anger from off Jeremiah's neck, crying, "Even so will the Lord break the yoke of the King of Babylon!"

But Jeremiah made answer: "Thou hast broken the yoke of wood, but thou shalt make for this people yokes of iron. Hear, now, Hananiah: The Lord hath not sent thee; thou makest this people to trust in a lie. Therefore thus saith the Lord: 'This year thou shalt surely die.' "

So Hananiah, the prophet, died in that same year.

And in the tenth month, the tenth day of the month, came Nebuchadnezzar with all his host and pitched against Jerusalem and built forts round about. And Nebuchadnezzar besieged the city till Pharaoh came up out of Egypt. Then Nebuchadnezzar withdrew to give battle to Pharaoh Hophra; and the people rejoiced in Jerusalem, saying: "The war is over!"

Nevertheless, Jeremiah said: "Do not deceive yourselves. The enemy will return; for though ye had smitten the whole of the Chaldean host, and there remained but wounded men among them, yet should they rise up every man in his tent and burn this city with fire."

And Jeremiah went forth to dwell for a time apart; but at the city-gate, I-ri'jah, captain of the watch, stopped him roughly and said: "Thou goest to join the Chaldeans."

And Irijah brought him to the princes, and the princes put him in prison in the house of Jonathan, the scribe.

But when some days were gone, the Chaldeans came again, as Jeremiah had said, and laid siege to Jerusalem; for they had defeated Pharaoh. Then Jeremiah said: "He that remaineth in this city shall die, but he that goeth forth to the Chaldeans shall live." Thus he spake as beforetime.

And the princes went to the king and said: "We beseech

Assyrians besiege a city on a hill, possibly Jerusalem. (Assyrian carving) For Pharaohs Hophra and Necho, see Vol. II, p. 248.

Ebed-melech, the Ethiopian eunuch, draws Jeremiah up from the pit of mire. King Zedekiah, the weakling, stood in real awe of Jeremiah and wanted to help him, but was always afraid of the princes.

thee, let this man be put to death; for he weakeneth the hands of the men of war in speaking such words unto them."

And Zedekiah said weakly: "Behold, he is in your hands, for the king is not he that can do anything against you."

So they took Jeremiah and cast him into a dungeon that was in the court of the prison; and they let him down with cords. And in the dungeon there was no water but mire.

Now when E'bed-me'lech, the Ethiopian, one of the King's eunuchs, heard what they had done, he ran to Zedekiah, then sitting in the gate of Benjamin, and said: "My lord the king, these men have cast Jeremiah into a pit; and he is like to die of hunger."

And the King commanded Ebed-melech, saying: "Take him thence."

So Ebed-melech took thirty men and went into the King's house under the treasury and took thence old cast-off rags and let them down by cords into the pit to Jeremiah.

And Ebed-melech said: "Put these soft rags under thine armholes under the cords."

And Jeremiah did so; and they drew him up and he abode in the court of the prison till the day that the city was taken.

And Zedekiah at times sent secretly to fetch him thence that he might seek advice at his mouth; but he never had courage to follow his words. "I am afraid," he said; "afraid of the Jews lest they mock me!"

Nevertheless, in those days when the worst was come to pass, the old man, Jeremiah, straitly shut up in prison, dreamed, as Isaiah had dreamed, of a savior to come to Judah, a King of the line of David, who should rule the world in righteousness. He dreamed of a world made happy and free, singing in the height of Zion, flowing together to the goodness of the Lord, sorrowing no more at all.

And he spake his visions of comfort in the ears of all the Jews that sat in the court of the prison. And to show the certainty of his faith, that the Jews would return to Judah, he publicly bought of his cousin a field then overrun by the vast Chaldean host. He weighed out the money and said:

"Houses and fields and vineyards shall be possessed again in this land, whereof ye say, 'It is desolate, it is given to the Chaldean.'

"Again shall be heard in this place the voice of joy and the voice of gladness, the voice of the bridegroom and the voice of the bride!

"Thus saith the Lord: 'In those days I will make this covenant with Israel: I will put my law in their inward parts and write it in their hearts!'"

Jeremiah weighs out the money to buy of his cousin Ha-nam'e-el the field then overrun by Chaldeans, that thereby he may encourage his people to believe the fields of Judah will again be possessed by Jews.

And the city was besieged unto the eleventh year of King Zedekiah; but in those days there was no more bread, and the city was broken up. And all the princes of Babylon came and sat in the Middle Gate. And when Zedekiah saw them, he fled with his men of war, and they went forth out of the city by night, by way of the King's Gardens, by the gate betwixt the two walls. But the Chaldeans pursued them and overtook Zedekiah racing in his chariot across the plain of Jericho, and they brought him to Nebuchadnezzer at Rib'leh on the O-ron'tes.

Then the King of Babylon slew the sons of Zedekiah before his eyes. He also slew all the nobles of Judah. Moreover he put out Zedekiah's eyes and bound him with chains to carry him to Babylon. And he sent his servant Neb'u-zar-a'dan, captain of the guard, to Jerusalem. And Nebuzara-

Zedekiah flees by night through the gate between the old wall of David and the later wall of Hezekiah, and down across the green patches of kitchen garden called the King's Gardens, to escape to Jericho.

Zedekiah and his sons are brought before Nebuchadnezzar at Riblah on the Orontes. See page 83.

dan burnt the House of the Lord and the king's house and all the houses of Jerusalem and brake down the walls round about. And the pillars of brass that were before the temple, and the bases, and the brazen sea, did he break in pieces and carried the brass thereof to Babylon. And all the vessels of the temple and such things as were of gold and silver did the captain of the guard take away, and all the best of the people, saving only a miserable remnant, poor husbandmen and vine-dressers, left to till the soil.

But Nebuzaradan took Jeremiah out of the court of the prison and set him free, because he had counselled submission unto King Nebuchadnezzar. And Nebuzaradan said unto Jeremiah: "Go where it seemeth good unto thee. If thou wilt come to Babylon, I will look well unto thee."

But Jeremiah refused the ease and comfort of Babylon. For the great love he bare his people, he chose to remain with the remnant. And he saw Jerusalem desolate, a blackened heap of ruins, she that was called "the perfection of beauty, the joy of the whole earth." He saw her children crying for bread, her people swooning for hunger. And he cried from the depths of his sorrow:

Ah, how the city sits solitary; she that was full of people!
Ah, how she sits as a widow; she that was great among nations!
A princess among the provinces; how is she tributary!

Behold how she weepeth in darkness; tears on her cheeks are falling;
Behold, among all her lovers, none there are left to comfort;
Basely her friends become traitors, bitter foes to her greatness!

Captive the land of Judah because of her affliction, because of
        her great oppression!
Captive she dwells among heathen; nowhere can she find resting.
Crying, her persecutors, come crowding to overtake her.

Deep mourn the ways of Zion; deserted her solemn assemblies,
Desolate are her gates; her priests are dreary with sighing.
Desolate are her virgins; in bitterness is she dwelling.

Enemies dare to rule her; her adversaries do prosper;
Evil hath fallen upon her, for the multitude of her transgressions;
Even her little children, are taken away as captives.

From the fair daughter of Zion, her majesty is departed;
Fleeing like harts, her princes nowhere find them a pasture,
Forth have they fared without strength, fleeing before the pursuer.

The Lamentations of Jeremiah is written in acrostics, the various stanzas beginning with successive letters of the
alphabet and featuring that letter. Hebrew poetry had no rhyme but often used acrostics and repetition of phrases.

Obadiah the prophet, in the days of Judah's trouble, sees the Edomites come down from their cliffs and stand at the cross-ways among the green terraced hills of Jerusalem's countryside, to cut off escaping Jews and deliver them back to Babylon.   The book of Obadiah is one long grievous outcry against the people of Edom.

And in the day when the stranger carried off Judah captive, Edom came down from her cliffs and stood on the side of Babylon. Her folk rejoiced over Judah. They entered the gates of Jerusalem and laid hands on her substance. They shed the blood of her children. They stood at the cross-ways to cut off those that escaped and deliver them back to Babylon. And O'ba-di'ah, the prophet, cried in anger against them:

"Thou that dwellest in the clefts of the rock, whose habitation is high, that saith in his heart: 'Who shall bring me down?' 'though thou exalt thyself as an eagle, and though thou set thy nest among the stars, thence will I bring thee down,' saith the Lord."

But Jeremiah found comfort; and he said to himself: "It is good that a man should both hope and quietly wait for the salvation of the Lord. He doth not afflict willingly nor grieve the children of men. Let us search and try our ways and turn again to the Lord."

Ishmael the outlaw, and his wild robber band slay Gedaliah, governor of Judah, as they celebrate the feast.

Now Nebuchadnezzar left, as governor over Judah, Ged'-a-li'ah, a Jew, grandson of Shaphan, the scribe, the friend of Jeremiah; and Jeremiah went and joined himself unto Gedaliah at Mizpah; and thither were brought for safety the daughters of Zedekiah, who had escaped the butchery whereby their brothers were slain; and thither came all the Jews who had fled round-about for refuge.

But Ish'ma-el, an outlaw, a wild unruly fellow, born of the princes of Judah, had fled across the Jordan to Ba'al-is, King of Ammon. And Ba'al-is hired Ishmael and his free-booting robber band to go and slay Gedaliah.

And Jo-ha'nan, captain of Judah's host, came and warned Gedaliah, but the governor, nothing heeding, made a feast for Ishmael; whereat the band of Ishmael secretly rose and slew him, his household, and his men.

Then they went down to the town, took captive the sad young princesses with their eunuchs and all the people, and started to make off to Ammon.

Hotly Johanan pursued them. Two of Ishmael's band he slew; the people he delivered; and Ishmael himself he forced to flee at topmost speed to seek the shelter of Ammon.

Then Johanan and the people feared lest Nebuchadnezzar should say: "The Jews committed this murder. Punish them severely!" And they thought to flee into Egypt.

But Jeremiah said: "Flee not; for ye have done no wrong!"

Nevertheless, the people would not obey Jeremiah; they took the old man and the princesses, and fled across the desert, till they saw rising up from the low mud-swamps and heron-haunted lagoons, the tall square tower of Daph'nae, a frontier fortress of Egypt, where dwelt Pharaoh Hophra's mercenaries, hired soldiers from Greece.

The sad young princesses, daughters of Zedekiah, in company with Jeremiah, flee into Egypt. They see before them Tahpanhes, and the hired Greek soldiers of Pharaoh Hophra. Jeremiah is carried to Egypt much against his will; for he has warned the people that they have done no harm and would not need to flee.

Greek figures such as Jeremiah must have seen on the streets of Tahpanhes, an old man, two dancers, and a dancing girl from paintings on Greek vases found at Tahpanhes. Later Pharaohs hired many Greek soldiers. (V.I, 247.)

And Hophra sent word to the princesses to use the tall square palace, and the Arabs call it to this day: "The Castle of the Jews' Daughters."

And the Jews settled down in Egypt. But in the stubbornness of their hearts, they once again burned incense unto the Queen of Heaven. And they said: "When we worshipped the Queen of Heaven we had enough to eat and were well and saw no evil. Let us worship her again."

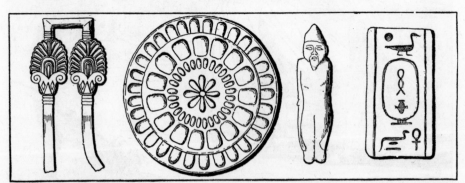

A golden tray handle inlaid with color, which was part of a gold tray that may very probably have been used by the two exiled princesses to whom Pharaoh Hophra gave the use of rooms in the tower; a limestone cake-mould in which perhaps cakes were baked for the princesses; a rude, little stone figure of a captive (Hebrew perhaps) with which the Greek soldiers at Tahpanhes played a game, lined out on the sand; and the plaque of Pharaoh Hophra himself. All these were found at Tahpanhes or Daphnae, as the Greeks called it.

Jeremiah rebukes the Jews to the last days of his life, while the Greeks of Tahpanhes look on.   The brickwork before the tower under which the Bible says Jeremiah buried the stones, has been discovered at Tahpanhes.

Even here, in these last days of trouble, Jeremiah was forced to cry, as he had all the years of his life: "No good ever came from serving the Queen of Heaven. It was because you worshipped her that this evil has come upon you."

And he laid great stones beneath the brickwork pavement of the tower, thundering forth stern reproaches: "Ye disobeyed God in fleeing; for He bade you remain in Judah. But ye shal! not, through disobedience, escape from Nebuchadnezzar! He will follow you hither and set up his throne on these stones."

Staunchly the old man stood, ceaselessly proclaiming, in spite of all his weary years of bitter disappointment, that real peace can come only from cleansing the heart and spirit; from inner purification and obedience to God.

But the people said: "We will not hearken to thee; we will certainly do as we please." And they went on making cakes to worship the Queen of Heaven.

And the fire-burned ruins of Daphnae with a cylinder of Nebuchadnezzar found in the blackened heap, show that Nebuchadnezzar did, indeed, destroy Daphnae, set up his throne on the stones, and chasten the Jews again.

Ezekiel, the Scholar, the Watchman of the Captivity

For seventy years the captives languished in sorrow in Babylon, ever longing for home and the pleasant places of Judah; and they sang from the depths of their grief:

> By the rivers of Babylon there we sat down,
> Yea, we wept when we remembered Zion.
> We hanged our harps upon the willows in the midst thereof;
> For there they that carried us away captive,
>   Required of us a song;
>   And they that wasted us, required of us mirth,
>   Saying: "Sing us one of the songs of Zion."
> How shall we sing the Lord's song in a strange land?

And before the fall of Jerusalem, their hope rose ever anew that Judah would smite the tyrant, and they should soon go home. And the false prophets said as heretofore: "Your captivity will be short."

And the people believed their words and followed their old evil ways, setting up idols in Babylon even as they had in Judah.

But there dwelt with the captives in Babylon a friend of Jeremiah's, Ezekiel, the priest, a student and a scholar, who had gone with the first train of exiles. And Ezekiel dwelt with his wife in an house on the river Che'bar; and he stood as a watchman unto his people, speaking the plain, unpopular truth against the lying prophets.

And when the false prophets said: "Judah will soon be victorious," Ezekiel got himself forth into a public street. He took a tile and built a mimic city upon it. He took sticks and stones and built a mimic fort, and a mimic camp, and set up toy battering rams round about. Moreover, he took an iron pan and set it up for a wall. And when a crowd had gathered to see what he was about, he cried:

"Thus saith the Lord: 'This is Jerusalem.'"

Ezekiel builds a mimic city as he dwells among the exiles in Babylon, and when his people draw near, he destroys his city before them all, to show what is soon to be the fate of Jerusalem. Ezekiel, though much younger, was a friend of Jeremiah's, and he carried on in Babylon the work that Jeremiah did in Judah, urging his people to inner cleansing of mind and spirit as the only way to safety, happiness and peace. He dwelt much, too, on the fact that each man is responsible for himself alone. "The son," he said, "shall not bear the iniquity of the father, neither shall the father bear the iniquity of the son; but each shall be rewarded according to his own doings." Ezekiel spoke much in figures and drove his points home by acting out dramatic signs and symbols.

And Ezekiel smote his city and destroyed it before them all.
And he went unto his house and brought forth all his household stuff in the sight of all the people, bearing it on his shoulders as one that goes into captivity, and he said:

"So shall they of Jerusalem remove and go into captivity. Cast away from you all your transgressions and make you a new heart and a new spirit, for why will ye die, O house of Israel. For 'I have no pleasure in the death of him that dieth,' saith the Lord God. Wherefore turn yourselves, and live ye."

And the people came unto Ezekiel and sat before him and heard his words. With their mouth they showed much love, but their hearts went after their covetousness. They talked against Ezekiel by the walls, and in the doors of the houses. And lo, Ezekiel was unto them as a very lovely song of one that hath a pleasant voice and can play well on an instrument; for they heard his words but they did them not.

Nevertheless, Ezekiel was lifted above his grief by the splendor of dreams and visions,—the glory of God in brightness flashing across his thoughts, visions of fire and amber glow; of lamps and lightning and burning coals; of shining figures and sapphire thrones shedding the hues of the rainbow. So was he lifted up and carried away in dreams.

But now in the last sad days before Jerusalem fell, the

Ezekiel was a man of visions, of visions sometimes confused but always fiery and glorious. His mind was aflame with a keen, stupendous sense of the glory of God and he thought of that flaming glory as an amber cloud of brightness surrounding a sapphire throne, about which attendant cherubim flew gleaming like burnished brass, the noise of their wings like great waters. These cherubim of his dreams each having four faces, one of a man, one of a lion, one of an ox and one of an eagle, though their outward form was doubtless shaped from the winged bulls and lions of Babylon, expressed the brilliance and courage, the strength and swift easy movement of those winged thoughts in the heart of man that wait on the glory of God.

wife of Ezekiel died; the desire of his eyes was taken away at a stroke; but he neither wept nor mourned with outward show of mourning; for he bound his head-dress upon him and put his shoes on his feet and walked abroad as aforetime. And the people wondered and said: "Why cometh Ezekiel forth, making no sign of mourning?"

And Ezekiel answered and said: "I do this for a sign; for there cometh on you likewise a sorrow too deep for mourning. So shall Jerusalem, the joy of thy glory, be taken away from thee."

And one that had escaped out of Jerusalem came and said: "The city is smitten."

Then Ezekiel gathered his people together and gave them comfort, saying:

"Behold, Judah is as an heap of dry bones in the midst of a valley; but the spirit of God as the breath of wind shall enter these bones, and they shall rise up and live. Thus saith the Lord: 'From all your filthiness will I cleanse you. And ye shall dwell in the land that I gave unto your fathers.' "

So Ezekiel stood as a watchman guarding the truth for his people, and after him rose others, even such as Daniel, and that tender, Unknown Comforter, who left no name behind, because his words were copied into the Book of Isaiah, he who cries so compassionately from the fortieth chapter and onward: "Comfort ye, comfort ye, my people, saith your God."

These men and the sacred books, far greater in number now than they had been before in the days of the prophet, Isaiah, kept the knowledge of God alive in the hearts of the sorrowing captives. Slowly those homesick wanderers, the flower of the people of Judah, ceased their most glaring sins. In the long weary days of exile, they cast their idols aside, and came, as a race, to acknowledge, at last, the one God of Israel.

Prince Zerubbabel, in the softly draped Persian costume of his days of exile, encourages the people to rebuild their homes and the temple. He is aided by the prophet Haggai and the prophet Zechariah, who loved beauty and the laughter of children and the merry bells of the horses. For the conquest of Babylon by the Persians see page 85.

The Return of the Captives to Judah

Now in Daniel's latter days, Cyrus, the Persian, came and laid siege to Babylon, and took it and made himself king in Babylon. (538 B.C.) And Cyrus had no mind to grind down captive peoples. He sent as many Jews as wished, under their Prince Ze-rub′ba-bel of the royal line of Judah, back to the City of David to build the temple anew.

And the people built themselves houses and labored to build the temple, encouraged by Zech′a-ri′ah and Hag′ga-i, the prophets.

And Haggai said: "Be strong, O Zerubbabel; be strong, all ye people and work; for I am with you, saith the Lord!"

And Zechariah cried, his spirit bright as a raincloud, promising showers of refreshment: "Sing and rejoice, O daughter of Zion. The Lord your God will save you; for how great is his goodness and how great is his beauty! There shall yet old men and old women dwell in the streets of Jerusalem; the city shall be full of boys and girls playing in the streets thereof; and in that day, shall be written on all the bells of the horses: 'Holiness unto the Lord!'"

So Judah remained a province subject unto Persia. But after an hundred years, in 445 B.C., Ne'he-mi'ah, the Jew, cup-bearer to Ar'ta-xer'xes, heard how miserable still were his people back in Judah, because their city lay without walls open to every foe; and he got permission to go as governor of the land. By night, he rode out on an ass and sorrowed over the fallen walls and the gates that were burned with fire. And thereafter he urged the people to build the walls anew.

Then San-bal'lat, the Samaritan, with To-bi'ah, the Ammonite, and others who hated to see Jerusalem rise again in strength, mocked at him and said: "What do these feeble Jews? Do they think to give life to an heap of rubbish?"

And they said to the men on the walls: "We will come and slay thee, and cause this work to cease!"

Sanballat, the Samaritan, and Tobiah, the Ammonite, mock at Nehemiah and the Jews as they rebuild the wall.

Therefore Nehemiah made a prayer to his God and set a watch against them; and they that labored on the wall wrought with one hand in the work and held in the other a weapon. And Nehemiah rested not; neither did he, nor his servants, nor his brethren, nor the men of the guard which followed him, put off their clothes, save that everyone put them off for washing.

Then Sanballat and Tobiah tried to trick Nehemiah, sending him a message to urge him down from the walls, that they might secretly slay him; but he answered them only thus: "I am doing a great work. Why should I come down to thee?" And naught could tempt him down.

And Ezra, the scribe, aided Nehemiah, and began the business of gathering together the sacred books of the Jews.

And when the walls were done, all the people came as one man, thronging unto the place before the Water Gate. And Ezra, the scribe, stood on a pulpit of wood, built for the purpose, high above them all, and he read to the people from the book of the law of the Lord. And the people lifted up their hands and bowed their heads, and worshiped the Lord. And Ezra read the book distinctly, and gave the sense and caused the people to understand the reading. And Nehemiah said: "This day is holy unto our Lord. Be glad in it and rejoice; for the joy of the Lord is your strength."

And all the people made mirth because they had understood the words of the law. And they went and fetched olive branches and palm branches and made booths in the streets and dwelt in them for a season. And there was very great gladness.

So the Old Testament ends, the people faithful at last to one God, and following His law with real understanding.

The Hebrews gave the world no gifts of art or architecture, of organization or government. They were a little nation, small and unimportant in the outward paths of history, but they gave the human heart its greatest inspiration, sympathetic knowledge of one vital, living God, whose power is the life of the universe and the urge to everything good within the hearts of men. The Greeks sought perfection in beauty; the Hebrews sought it in righteousness. Though the mass of people never rose to the heights of their greatest men, their knowledge of God increased with every generation. With each new spiritual seer, God's nature of goodness and beauty, of round and whole perfection, was ever more clearly seen, and man's assurance of lasting joy in striving to be perfect even as God is perfect.

Ezra the scribe, reading the words of the Bible to the people. Ezra did much to help in gathering together the sacred books of the Old Testament, aiming to inspire his people again with some national life and spirit.

Parts of the Book of Kings are among the oldest material in the Bible. These public records were kept in the time when the acts narrated took place, but were worked over and edited, and did not take final form until about 550 B.C., in the days of exile in Babylon.

The books of the prophets took shape about the time of the prophets, but the Pen'ta-teuch or first five books of the Bible, (Genesis, Exodus, Leviticus, Numbers and Deuteronomy), though they have much old material, doubtless dating back to Moses, were not put in final form until the time of Ezra, when Joshua and Judges were also re-edited, and the Book of Chronicles gathered together, a much later work than Kings. The Old Testament was originally in Hebrew, but after the return from exile, Aramaic became the language of common speech. The oldest edition of the Old Testament in existence today, is written in Greek. It was made by the Jews in Alexandria about 280 B.C., and is called the Sep'tu-a-gint.

INDEX

INDEX

KEY TO PRONUNCIATION

ā as in māte	ä as in färm	ĭ as in ĭt	ū as in mūte
ă as in căt	ē as in ēve	ō as in mōte	ŭ as in cŭt
â as in câre	ĕ as in lĕt	ŏ as in nŏt	ōō as in fōōd
á as in ásk	ī as in mīnd	ô as in nôr	ŏŏ as in fŏŏt